Adolescence and its Significance
for those with Special Needs

ADOLESCENCE
AND ITS SIGNIFICANCE
FOR THOSE WITH SPECIAL NEEDS

Including three essays by
Karl König

Compiled and edited by
Michael Luxford

Camphill Books

Camphill Working Papers on Adolescence Volume I
First published 1983
2nd edition revised and enlarged 1995

Published by TWT Publications Ltd.
on behalf of
The Youth Guidance Group,
Centres of the Camphill Movement in Great Britain
for young people with special needs

British Library CIP Data
A catalogue record for this book is available from the British Library

ISBN 1 897839 11 1

This publication has been assisted by:
Youth Guidance Course,
Camphill Foundation U.K.

MADE AND PRINTED IN GREAT BRITAIN
BY CAMPHILL PRESS, BOTTON VILLAGE,
DANBY, WHITBY, NORTH YORKSHIRE YO21 2NJ

Acknowledgements

The editor wishes to thank Veronika van Duin, Sandra Stoddard, Penny West, and Andrew Shackleton of Asgard Publishing Services, for their advice and helpful comments made during preparation of the text, and Wain Farrants and Nicholas Poole of Botton Village for their practical help and forbearance during the lengthy editing process. The editor also wishes to thank the Trustees of the Karl König Archive for permission to publish the essays by him found at the end of this volume.

Contents

Three Essays on Adolescence

Dr. Karl König

Introduction

It is almost twelve years since I sat down to write the introduction to the first edition of this volume on adolescence. At that time I had the image of the pink-haired punk rocker on my mind. I remember being at Charing Cross Station in London one summer evening and seeing a group of such wildly coloured youths standing in the middle of the concourse while sober, grey-suited mainstream commuters edged nervously past them, trying not to notice these aliens!

Twelve years on, I asked a few young people of the 1990s to talk about being young. It wasn't easy to get the conversation going. No verbal 60s rebels or extreme nihilistic acid-freaks, but a group of fine, intelligent people. What did they say?

Today, in the West, education is extended for as long as possible because there are no jobs. You become uncertain, doubtful and feel a lot of pressure. There isn't any interest in politics and the environment. You can't do much except be environmentally friendly and buy only certain products.

If you live in an Eastern European country where you have to pull the country into the future, then you can find motivation. If you live in Israel, you have to spend three years of your life in the army, have no choice, and discover humiliation and what it means to be a nothing. When there are no jobs and no great enemies, you begin to feel superfluous, not needed, and then it doesn't matter if you are there or not. But you are, and so one answer is to fill the vacuum with excitement, with distraction.

Maybe the reader will have recognised some of the characteristics of the young people of today in the above observations. In a different form I believe the punk–stockbroker divide still exists. It is found between the glitzy world of Thatcher's successful children who made it into employment and possessions, good clothes, holidays, style and views, and those who, despite their hedonistic pursuits, are amazingly kind, decent and admirable. What will capitalism do when it discovers that these youngsters don't give a damn for fashion clothes, cannot be hyped, will live simply and do not have the Darwinian streak of ambition for image? Perhaps there are only a few of them, as yet, next to the thousands of football fans and flashy dressers, but, like those before them, the few identify and describe the times.

* * * * *

The articles in this book span almost 40 years. Almost without exception they derive from individuals who have lived and worked in the Camphill Movement and from people who have had a long-standing interest in young people, and particularly those with special needs.

The archetype of adolescence is described in different ways in the first selection of articles and lectures under the heading of Adolescence. The next two contributions are on Training in Adolescence for those with special needs. Even though they were written around 30 years ago, it is amazing how relevant they are to the work-training situation of today. Finally, there are Three Essays on Adolescence by Dr Karl König, the founder of the Camphill Movement. They are included because I regard them as excellent examples of courageous research, of which there is too little today. We have to be careful about what we say, yet here Dr König uses his creativity to try to discover the truth underlying various phenomena. Nowadays we seem to be so bland and unimaginative compared with him.

Although what is found here may sometimes seem dated, it is nonetheless still relevant to the world of today. I regard what is printed here as building stones, placed there by enthusiasts who did not wish to skirt around young people, but to walk up to them and ask, 'How are you and where are you going?' Hopefully, this collection will be of use to the reader, offering further angles from which to view this complex yet crucial phase of life and the challenges it presents to the less-able person.

Michael Luxford
Pennine Community
1st June 1995

Editorial note:
The authors of these articles made regular use of the pronoun 'he' to refer to both male and female, whereas writers nowadays prefer to use more inclusive expressions. However, to edit the text along modern inclusive principles would make the style awkward and cumbersome, so we have not attempted to change this.

Adolescence

Adolescence

Anke Weihs

from *The Cresset* vol. 16 no 3, 1970

The word adolescence is derived from the Latin *adolescere* meaning 'to grow into adulthood'. The term is applied generally to the period between 14 and 21, which is the third seven-year period of life. The first period up to the age of seven marks the end of infancy and early childhood; the second, ending at 14, sees a child into puberty; and the third, which ends at the 21st year, marks the beginning of adulthood. The earlier phases have admittedly become shorter and faster nowadays, simply because children tend to grow up much more quickly. But the fundamental characteristics of the three periods remain unchanged.

If the third seven-year period of life is one of growing into adulthood, then this means it is a process that is not yet active at birth. This in turn implies that childhood is a state in its own right, and not merely an initial stage preparatory to becoming adult. Childhood can thus be seen as a well-defined, self-contained, universal state with its own laws of growth and organic development; future expectations and demands should not be allowed to impinge upon it.

The two seven-year periods that make up childhood can be viewed as two sides of the same coin. The first period begins with birth — the separation of an infant's body from that of his mother. The second period begins with a certain landmark in biological growth when a child's mind can start to develop; by this stage he will already have started school. In a sense, this second step might be called a 'second birth' — a mental birth.

In the same sense, one could say that a growing child has two further 'births' ahead of him. The 'third birth' is the separation of his emotional life from that of his parents and family. His relationships and responses become his own, and are no longer just determined by those of his family background — he becomes emotionally independent. This change culminates some time around his 14th year.

The fourth and final 'birth' in the development of a young person is that of his ego. This is the point when he achieves a working relationship with his own self as a separate entity apart from all other individuals.

Thus the first three seven-year periods of life can be seen as successive 'pregnancies', each culminating in a 'birth'. Only after all these 'births' have been completed is a person fully 'born' as an individual.

Let us return to childhood for a moment. Childhood is a distinct sphere of physical and biological growth. A child already has the potential for emotional independence and individuality; these elements of his future adulthood seem to play around his childhood state, just as the wind, weather and sunlight play over the fertile earth. But the world of childhood is soon to be invaded by the dynamic power of the child's own emotional 'weather'. He begins to have his own personal 'climate', as distinct from that of his surroundings.

As the growing youth becomes aware of the climate around him — classically at the age of 14 — so he enters the period of adolescence. Adolescence begins with puberty, but this is not to say that the two are the same thing. On the contrary, there is in fact a vital distinction between adolescence and puberty.

Adolescence is a new *beginning*, marked by the 'third birth' described above: the young person sets off into unexplored territory under a new set of conditions. It is the beginning of of an individual's spiritual development, and therefore is essentially forward-looking.

Puberty, on the other hand, is the *end* of something — the culmination of various biological processes that have been going on since conception. To take a botanical analogy, a plant's development starts with germination; the plant then sprouts, develops leaves and flowers, ripens and is eventually ready to seed. In a sense, a human being at puberty is like a plant that is ready to seed. Puberty is the end of childhood — the natural end of a natural process — and in this sense it is backward-looking.

The fact that puberty and adolescence come together at the same time creates one of the major turning points in human development. The first of these occurred between the first and second years of life, when the infant suddenly became aware of his own ego: all at once he began to refer to himself as 'I', at a time when he was insufficiently developed and entirely ill-equipped to deal with himself as an individual. We know from the histories of many children with special needs how vulnerable a child is at this particular moment in life. Likewise, the point where puberty and adolescence meet is another dangerous moment when a growing youth becomes especially vulnerable.

How much safer human life would be if puberty could only wait until after adolescence! How much more harmonious life would be if a person's first experience of his own ego were only as the culmination of his first 21 years of development! Man was no more than a puppet of the gods when Prometheus wrested him from his pre-ordained state of serene perfection, and conferred upon man his own Promethean lot. The culmination of puberty arrives too soon, and the beginning of adulthood comes afterwards, troubled by what has already taken place. Natural and spiritual development are pitted against one another. Nothing fits. Everything is at odds. Like Prometheus bound, the growing human mind or soul is fettered to the precipitous rock of existence — a prey to the anger of the gods, endangered yet resilient, helpless yet in possession of a secret the gods themselves fear. Such is the secret of man's advance towards a perfection of his own through moral suffering and moral striving.

Only when a young person has reached adulthood do these apparently mistimed aspects of his growth and development begin to fall into step, or at least to enter into some kind of co-existence.

To sum up, then, adolescence is a human state, puberty a biological one. Puberty normally occurs as the young person enters adolescence, but the two are not the same thing. Puberty is confined to a definite period, whereas adolescence, as a state of growing into adulthood, can linger on into adulthood proper.

* * * * *

If adolescence is to be understood as a purely human state, this would mean that animals have no transitional adolescent phase between puberty and adulthood. We therefore speak of either a young animal or a mature animal. But to what extent is this true? Is there a phase in animal development equivalent to human adolescence?

In all the more highly organised animals, there are distinct phases of infancy and childhood that are reminiscent of human childhood. Take the polar-bear cub, for instance, with its enchanting and inventive mischief, or the play of the otter cub, the kitten, the puppy or the lion cub — each displaying infancy and childhood in its own delightful way. But there the resemblance ends. As soon as the polar-bear cub reaches physical maturity, all the deadly seriousness of a polar bear's existence weighs down heavily upon him. He enters an irrevocable adult state in which he is one of the fiercest and, to man, the most inaccessible of beasts. The relentless seriousness of animal life — of survival, procreation and protection of young — starts immediately with physical maturity.

The animal child and the human child appear to inhabit the same universal paradise of play. But with physical maturity the two part company — the animal to *be* what he is, the human being to *become* what he is meant to be. Adolescence as a state of *becoming* is reserved for human beings alone. As a consequence, it is both precarious and exquisite, dangerous and indispensable. Animals may pass through a phase that is apparently suggestive of adolescence, but this is really a phase of adaptation to given conditions, within which they exist but cannot advance — for they cannot taste the wine of the human ego.

* * * * *

Dr Karl König said that a newborn infant is wounded and shocked by his birth. It is not only the mother who labours, but the infant labours too, through the narrow passage that leads from the deepest security into the blinding light of day. This means, said Dr König, that a newborn infant needs weeks and months of nursing and convalescence.

In one of his lectures to the Camphill Movement[1], König spoke of an infant as being sick — not sick unto death, but unto life. He steadily recovers from this sickness as he grows and develops, and by the time he is seven years old, he has attained complete health. The child now enters one of the healthiest phases of his life. This does not mean that he is free from physical disease, but that there is balance and harmony between himself and the world around him. With the coming of puberty, said König, the young person becomes sick yet again. This time the sickness stems from the shock of physical maturity, and the recovery period is that of adolescence.

Puberty, like birth, is a moment of sickness. A child who was conceived and born in labour now becomes ready to conceive and bring forth in labour. Puberty puts him into an entirely new situation: he can participate in the mysteries of creation, which now lie within his power. Yet as a person he is not ready for this, since neither his identity nor his capacity for responsibility are sufficiently established. He has not yet grown into adulthood.

It would seem, therefore, that adolescence has two purposes to fulfil: a young person's recovery from the sickness of puberty, and an individual's growth from childhood into adulthood. Yet the second of these conflicts with the first. It is no wonder that adolescence is a period of extremes, and that as such it often proves intolerable for adults, who have long since completed their own adolescence.

* * * * *

The more ancient or unsophisticated a particular culture happens to be, the shorter is the transitional period between physical maturity and adulthood. In ancient tribal life, for instance, puberty rites marked the initiation of boys and girls into adulthood. Even today, in countries where there is still a peasant class, boys and girls tend to move relatively quickly from puberty into adulthood; the demands of the earth do not wait for the peasant to mature gently. In our society too, among certain underprivileged groups, boys and girls may often be children one day and adults the next. They cannot afford — whether financially or otherwise — to prolong their adolescence, but have to enter fairly quickly into responsible working life.

In older cultures, a youth of 14 was raised to the status of defender of the stronghold or city-state. In the Middle Ages, knighthood could be conferred on a youth of 14, and a young woman could have her first child at that age. Wolfram von Eschenbach in his great epic *Parzival* talks at great length about his hero's childhood and adulthood. Parzival's adolescence, on the other hand, effectively takes place during his ride from Arthur at Nantes to Gurnemanz's stronghold, where he becomes a man. Achilles, Siegfried, Theseus and other legendary heroes all end their childhood abruptly to fulfil their adult destiny. Only Telemachus is allowed a span of adolescence, because his father, Odysseus, although absent, is still king of Ithaca, and Telemachus is not yet fully responsible. If we turn to the Christian tradition, we find that St Luke's Gospel describes Jesus' life up to the age of 12, then continues from his 30th year. Likewise, John the Baptist appears as a child, then does not re-emerge until he is a man. There are two possible explanations for all this:

1   In earlier times much more value was attached to physical maturity out of a need to resist the pressures of external life; the need to *become* somebody as far as one's internal life was concerned would have seemed either incongruous or superfluous.

2   In earlier times the individual was not yet emancipated from the necessities of the city-state, fiefdom, clan or whatever. The state claimed its human material to fight its wars and suffer its vicissitudes regardless of age and maturity. It is as if the group had to be established before the individual could be established within the group. The Crusades are a good example of this. They swallowed up all males, young and old, and the females had to replenish the stock. Even children were drawn into the complex maelstrom of events associated with this period. There was no time for adolescence.

Especially among kings, the preservation of the line was of greater moment than an individual monarch's growth to maturity. James VI of Scotland (later James I of England) was crowned at the age of eight. Marriages among kings were made in infancy. The burden of the state rested upon the shoulders of children.

There was an exception to all this where crafts and guilds were concerned. No youth could become a master in a craft without first going through an apprenticeship. Apprenticeship in the crafts was the only form of adolescence in earlier times. Goethe in the first of his *Wilhelm Meister* novels, *Wilhelm Meister's Apprenticeship*[2], describes how his hero grows into adulthood (*Meister* means 'master', ultimately in the craft of life). It may well be that this influential novel was one of the factors that helped to establish adolescence as a legitimate and necessary phase of human development.

The Austrian writer Stifter also depicts a kind of adolescence or apprenticeship to life in his novel *Nachsommer*[3]. Henry, his hero, has to go through a higher school of nature, where he encounters geology, botany and (in a sublimated form) zoology, before finally reaching the House of the Roses, where he starts to fulfil his destiny as a man.

Goethe and Stifter were by no means the only figures of the eighteenth and nineteenth centuries to recognise adolescence as an inherent human state. For by this stage, man had at long last earned his adolescence.

The twentieth century is witnessing the mass proliferation of adolescence — so much so that psychologists are speaking of adolescents as a *new social class*. Adolescence begins earlier and lasts longer. The student, formerly an apprentice for a given period to his chosen profession, can maintain his status as student or apprentice indefinitely. One wonders sometimes if this clinging to adolescence is not a result of the curtailment of childhood, partly through early intellectual schooling and partly through the acceleration of growth in children. If a child is allowed to remain a child as long as he needs, with everything this implies, his growth into adulthood will not exceed its inherent span of time. If, however, he arrives at adolescence with a sense of having been deprived of a full childhood, he will do everything he can to prolong his juvenile status.

* * * * *

Now that we have considered some general aspects of adolescence, let us look at some of the same questions in relation to youngsters with special needs. Modern psychologists recognise three phases of adolescence which, to my mind, provide a workable basis for further deliberation:

- puberty — the biological phase;
- the search for identity — the psychological phase;
- coping — the social phase.

Clearly, the search for identity is the central phase, the core of adolescence, and hence the most crucial and vulnerable part. It is also the period of greatest increase in measurable intelligence. We are at our most intelligent during this middle phase of adolescence, and at the same time we are searching for our identity — part of the Promethean experience.

The search for identity can hardly be better described than by Tolstoy in the third part of his novel *Childhood, Boyhood and Youth*:

> At that period, which I regarded as the end of boyhood and the beginning of youth, my dreams were based on four feelings: love of her, the imaginary woman of whom I always dreamed in one and the same way, and whom I expected at any moment to meet somewhere. The second feeling was the love of being loved. I wanted everybody to know me and love me, I wanted to tell my name — and for everybody to be struck by this information, to surround me, and thank me for something. The third feeling was hope of some unusual, vainglorious good fortune. The fourth and chief feeling was self-disgust and repentance, but repentance so mingled with hope of happiness that it had nothing sad about it ... [4]

Youngsters with special needs have a tendency, like other unsophisticated groups, to move straight from puberty into some form of coping (i.e. with life in society to the extent that their limitations and capacities allow). However, this is not because they are potentially less sophisticated, but rather because their difficulties are revealed both in their measurable intelligence levels and in their search for identity.

In his lectures to the Camphill Movement[1], Dr König spoke of the 'masks' we wear in the many different life situations we encounter. Each situation calls for another 'mask' — in other words, a different aspect of our identity. Young people with special needs lack a certain pliability and adaptability when dealing with new situations. They choose a particular 'mask', which becomes fixed, regardless of changing demands.

This is particularly apparent among psychotic youngsters. After puberty they may seem to be coping relatively well, often showing astonishing skill and proficiency in certain types of work or craft. But coping requires more than just being able to work. It means being able to cope with oneself as a member of society, and we cannot achieve this if we have not established our identity.

Psychotic youngsters tend to bypass the search for identity. They may even run away from it or assiduously avoid it, so that they emerge from this phase with a shadow identity and illusory coping behaviour. There are all too many instances of youngsters who have sought perfection in work as a substitute for coping; this strategy has then been found wanting, leading to mental breakdown.

I should like to conclude with one vital question. What methods can we find to guide youngsters with special needs more effectively through these three phases of adolescence, and in particular through the central phase of identity-seeking? A sense of identity — the privilege of growing into adulthood — is the birthright of every human individual. How can we ensure that it is not bypassed and does not remain a missed opportunity? Herein lies an important challenge for us all.

The threshold of twenty-one

Rev. Julian Sleigh

from a lecture given in Camphill Soltane, USA, October 1991
In: *Journal for Curative Education and Social Therapy* summer 1994

In the case of young people with special needs, it is particularly important to focus on the 21st year of life when they cross the threshold from adolescence into adulthood. Several of the Camphill communities — notably the one at Soltane — have paid special attention to this transition, which can be so problematic for those who cannot readily take their place in the general, so-called normal, world of adult life. Dealing with this area of experience constitutes a discipline in itself, which is just as important as the two closely related fields of curative education and social therapy. The term most often used for this work is *youth guidance.*

A considerable body of experience, expertise and enterprise has already been accumulated in the area of youth guidance. This work is ongoing on a daily basis, meeting the many challenges that present themselves in the various communities. Regular seminars are held to talk over experiences and assess their significance, leading to a deeper understanding of this specialised field. The knowledge acquired can then be made available to others, providing enormous assistance in the development of the right methods and attitudes. It is greatly inspiring to watch this discipline grow, just as an adolescent grows through the transition from childhood to adulthood.

The vital question we must ask ourselves is this. If 21 is the normal age for a person to reach the milestone of adulthood, then what is the situation for the young person with special needs? If his development has been hampered by learning difficulties, physical disability, brain injury at birth or in early childhood, or a specific developmental abnormality such as Down's syndrome, how does this affect the timing of his adolescence?

But before answering this question, we should first examine the situation for the so-called normal person in the world of today.

The span of adolescence is nowadays thought to extend well outside the traditional parameters of ages 13 to 19. According to some people, adolescence often bursts into a child's world as early as nine, and stays with him right through until he is 22 or 23. This means that, instead of six or seven rumbustuous years, parents have to prepare for twice that number.

The time of true adolescence begins in the soul with the release of the astral forces (a term explained by Hans Heinrich Engel in his chapter *Thoughts and experiences with adolescents*). This has normally been reckoned to begin with the teens. The fact that adolescent behaviour appears earlier has to do with the collapse of childhood in our over-stressed Western culture. True adolescence — the awakening of the astral forces — usually waits for the teens. This is followed by the development of the ego, or individual personality, which at 21 becomes free to begin the task of taking responsibility for a person's behaviour and destiny.

When development has been impaired anything can happen. The adolescent period can be very brief, falling too soon or too hastily into a kind of 'heaviness', meaning that the flame of the personality can burn for a while, only to be overwhelmed by the physical growth of a prematurely adult body. We then have to try to coax the personality to re-emerge and take possession of the physical body and the soul forces. The adolescent needs encouragement to become a person in spite of himself. Otherwise he will remain a child in his soul long after puberty has set in, and his adolescence will extend far beyond the threshold of 21. He will be unable to gain control of his emotions or take initiative and responsibility. Without well-structured guidance, the transition to adulthood will simply not happen.

Motive forces

The life of the soul is like a stage on which three actors play out their roles. Karl König in his book *The Human Soul* [5] describes these three 'actors' as shame, fear and anger. If they balance each other, none of them can dominate. But if they do not, then one of the three may take over. This is something that affects all young people, but it applies all the more strongly to those with special needs as they approach the threshold of 21. If their development has been weakened in any way, then their state of mind as they enter adulthood can be all the more decisive. If one of the three 'actors' dominates, a person with special needs will not only be developmentally handicapped, but will be predisposed to further developmental problems in adulthood. In later life, moreover, such problems could easily contribute to the onset of mental illness.

This means there are two particular aims that a social therapist should endeavour to achieve in the case of young people with special needs:

1   to continually monitor and adjust their current life situations so as reduce the effect of any developmental dysfunction;

2   to ensure that in later life the ageing process does not trigger the onset of mental illness.

My own observations have led me to a number of conclusions.

Firstly, a young person who is driven by *shame* can easily succumb to 'heaviness', so that with the onset of adolescence he becomes sluggish in soul, or body, or both. The shame element is paralysing, manifesting itself in joylessness and lack of motivation. Such behaviour is usually described as lethargy or laziness. There are numerous examples of Down's syndrome children who have turned into sluggish, disgruntled young adults because the shame factor has become too strong. These young people find it difficult to apply themselves to learning new skills; there is little motivation to be active, and their earlier joyfulness drains away into nothing.

I am not referring here to shame in a moralistic sense, such as being ashamed at having done something wrong, but of something we all carry within us, and that we use to cover up the wounds we have received and the pain caused by them. The American psychotherapist John Bradshaw wrote a highly perceptive book on family dynamics, in which he described his observations on shame. He followed this with a penetrating book on the subject of shame itself.[6]

The second motive power in the soul is *fear*. This can lie at the root of the behaviour of people who become fixed into habits or even rituals. Such people derive security from routine, but they become dependent on that routine. We used to refer to children with this tendency as being 'pre-psychotic'. While the term is no longer accepted, it can be indicative of the kind of predisposition that may follow — for such children can become very fixed in their behaviour as adults.

The third strong force in the soul is *anger*. This is often caused by the frustration felt by a young person at being disabled in some way. He wants to do something but cannot. He sees his brothers and sisters moving on into life, and realises that he is probably never going to make that step himself. He contemplates a future in which he will remain dependent on what others provide for him. He sees himself as imprisoned, and adulthood for him provides no prospect of freedom and independence. Imagine being brain-damaged and being reminded of this every day — or every working hour of each day!

The task is to transform each of these powerful forces into something positive, so that creative energy can be helped to flow.

If a young person is burdened by shame, then he will need thorough training in a number of skills, and this despite any reluctance he may express. The primary aim is for him to be able to manage the various tasks competently. It is particularly important for the shame-driven person to acquire real proficiency in a variety of work skills.

If a person is overwhelmed by fear, then this fear needs to be properly met. He will need constant affirmation and reassurance in order to counteract the tendency to withdraw and refuse to communicate. Overwhelming loneliness can be transformed by warm, positive responses — in a word, friendship.

Someone who is fired by anger needs a dual approach. Firstly, he must learn to use his energies. He needs to be valuably employed so he can see the results of his work and feel he can achieve something in the world. Secondly, he must acquire some real culture. Usually the anger-driven person has a very poor soul life, with little imagination or sense of personal value. The world around him can seem bleak and meaningless. The introduction of cultural activity can help him start to cultivate a small oasis in the desert of his soul.

Any youth-guidance programme needs to contain these three vital elements: skill training, friendship and culture.

Biography and behaviour

When preparing young people for their entry into adulthood, it is also very important to examine both their life stories and their current behaviour.

One problem to look out for is that of *co-dependence*. The young person may be over-dependent on his mother or father, or they may be over-dependent on him. Co-dependence is an addictive state, in which an apparently close-knit family is in fact a rather tangled one. Does the young person turn to his parents for all the choices or decisions he has to make? Is the mother (less often the father) so absorbed in caring for him that neither she nor 'her child' is emotionally free of the other? If there is co-dependence, a recovery programme is needed, as with any addiction, or else the young person will be held back in his development. Being away from home is not enough, by itself, to repair the damage that has been done.

Closely connected with co-dependence is the question of whether a young person is heading for 'eternal childhood'. Is he likely to remain a child in the way he makes choices? Is he likely to remain dependent on guidance, or is he able to develop his own personal autonomy? Can he stand out from the crowd and hold his own point of view, set his own standards and keep to his own decisions? Is he able to think and act for himself, or does he simply react? One very strong indicator is the way a young person uses his spare time. Do his leisure activities require stimulation from outside, or can he work out his own forms of recreation? Would he, for example, decline to take part in a play or a game, and always opt instead for watching a film? Is he able to be himself as his ego develops? Or is he likely to remain imprisoned behind his one mask?

One very fruitful exercise is to ask the mother (and ideally the father, too) to write out the young person's life history as each of them recalls and feels it. This can help the parents to loosen the bonds, and it may also reveal the essential underlying causes of the young person's current behaviour and responses. Equipped with such a biography, the person giving guidance can go through it with the young person himself, who can either tell his own story or listen to his parents' biography and recall the events described. It will be significant which parts of the story he cannot remember, perhaps indicating a wish to blot them out. Or it may be apparent that he is clinging to a fantasy about his past prowess which he is obviously reluctant to let go. It is valuable for a person entering adulthood to become free of his own past. If he forgets something because he wishes to blot it out, he cannot be free until he has remembered it — and accepted it. If he is clinging to a fantasy, he will need to become reconciled to the illusory nature of his fantasy.

It is important to try to assess the young person's image of himself. You may think you know him well, but do you really know what he feels about himself, his mission in life, his burdens, his potential, his yearnings? To be open with a person in this way can help you to bond with him. For all young people, true friendship is as necessary as good nourishment. One-to-one conversations can bring healing to the fragile, hurting, perplexed personality within.

Companionship

There is a custom in some Camphill centres to refer to the young people as 'companions'. This is a good word, meaning that the young people also accompany those who are conventionally termed their carers or educators. The most important aspect of youth guidance is for those who are guiding them to seek to establish real companionship with the young people. The word 'companion' originally referred to people who shared the same bread: you share life, but you also share something of yourself. I have already spoken about the need to know the young people properly — their life history, the causes of their behaviour, and so on. But it is just as important for them to be able to get to know you — both your strengths and your weaknesses — and to know that you too are striving to deal with your own shortcomings. Then they will no longer see you as a model of perfection, but rather as an example of how to accept one's shortcomings but still keep on growing.

At this lonely time young people need friendship, but the coworker's task is to enable them to outgrow this dependence and find their own friends. Maybe in the end they will even be able to stretch out a helping hand to someone else who needs it. Meanwhile, they need more than just peer friendship — they need the encouraging support of people who can help them to put childish things behind them and take the step into adulthood.

This element of friendship is an important one. There are many people with special needs who become very lonely in later life. It is vital to find creative ways of helping them to make friends of their own, and the first step is to be their friends. But at the same time, guidance and companionship should not be allowed to cramp their initiative, or prevent opportunities for them to make their own choices.

Choice and adventure

It is good to have a programme which steadily increases each person's area of choice. In their teens — i.e. when the youth-guidance process begins — the young people need to abide by a disciplined framework. But by their early twenties this outward discipline should have been largely replaced by an inner discipline; then they are better able to handle the freedom that they are given.

There are all kinds of ways of providing choices. In the later years of the programme, for instance, the students can be allowed to help with planning their education curriculum. They can help plan their work and — most valuable of all — they can be encouraged to show initiative in the use of leisure and recreation time. They can decorate their rooms with their own personal effects, or select their own cultural pursuits. The cultural sphere provides ample opportunity for initiative, and helps them to develop a sense of responsibility. They might, for example, choose the songs to sing at a festival, or act as hosts for friends and neighbours who come for special occasions. The implication is that you are taking the young people seriously and recognising their potential.

During these years of transition through adolescence to adulthood, young people can benefit greatly from a good deal of adventure. This may be of the 'outward bound' variety, such as rafting down a river or climbing a mountain. But it can also be an adventure of the more inward kind, like preparing a play together in a way that stretches everyone's abilities and involvement. They need to discover a vibrant centre within their souls. If they can learn to tap this resource and give it expression, rather than just tag along with demands from other people, then this vibrant centre can begin to grow.

In the area of work, it is important that whatever is undertaken is real and demanding, for then it can draw upon each person's deeper resources and yield satisfaction. Finally, at the end of each day, they can be encouraged to look back at what they have achieved and to see that it is good. This, after all, was what God did after His days of creation. The activity of working in a team provides bonding — and people who work together can also pray together. However, work comes first — *labora et ora*.

By showing gratitude to today's young people, we can also engender a similar attitude in them. A person who cannot thank is miserable. Gratitude resounds with an inner music of its own, and it is good if young people can awaken to this. It is helpful, to begin with, if we can surround them with our gratitude.

* * * * *

In conclusion I would like to share with you one point which you probably know well, but which illustrates how people meet one another. It is the basic scheme of transactional analysis, as outlined in Thomas Harris' book *I'm OK — You're OK*[7]. In any relationship, *parent* (P) can be said to represent anyone in authority or power; *child* (C) represents anyone who submits; *adult* (A) is a person in his or her own right.

So often our relationships are P–C — or, for that matter, C–P. Every time you pigeon-hole another person in a role — 'priest', 'craft master', 'handicapped person' — you are in grave danger of relating P–C. Obviously the right situation is an A–A relationship. But in

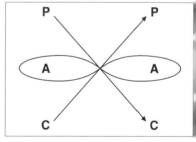

what circumstances can people relate to one another in an adult-to-adult fashion? Only when they avoid putting another person into any kind of box, but see him as he truly is. You yourself need to be prepared to be seen as a person, and not merely as a role. To achieve an A–A relationship, you need to overcome insecurity, vulnerability and strangeness, until the flow from person to person really begins to work.

What is this flow? I believe it is what we should call *feeling* (nothing to do with the feelings), and it is this that enables us to bond with each other in a healing way. This relationship is the one that is most helpful in a person whose ego is being formed. It doesn't only mean sitting down in a quiet room and having a one-to-one talk. It means generating a basic respect, interest and regard for the other's life situation.

* * * * *

The threshold of 21 heralds the birth of the ego — the true self. But this development needs space and it needs encouragement. This is the underlying motif of everything I have shared with you. There is the danger that people who have special needs and developmental difficulties become no more than co-operative automatons — which can look good and even feel good because it seems to make life easier. But if this happens, the true personality may have been stifled, while the astral forces, and the true soul development that stems from them, may have been hidden behind a convenient mask.

According to Karl König, the aim should be to help young people to develop many masks, and not to be limited to just one. When many masks are available, the astral forces are diffused, while the ego becomes actively engaged. The ego then has the task of selecting and presenting the mask that applies in a given situation. In an amazing way, Dr König points to the very core of what youth guidance is about.

The threshold of 21 is undoubtedly a significant milestone in a person's life — indeed, a major turning point in that person's life history. The beginning of adulthood opens the door to what can be the longest and most significant period of a person's life — twice as long as childhood and adolescence put together. Much depends on the way in which the young person has been prepared for this time. Youth guidance can make all the difference between a life of little significance and one in which a person can achieve the mission for which he came into the world.

The development of the soul in adolescence

Dr Susan Mechie

from a lecture given in the Pennine Community, England, May 1981

Adolescence extends roughly from the 13th or 14th year through to 20 or 21, although this varies between different individuals and cultural settings. It may be subdivided into three periods — given below as early, middle and late adolescence — although the three do overlap to some extent.

Adolescence has a different quality from previous phases of development. This is manifested in a wider and richer emotional life, and a tendency towards more inward experience and self-discovery. The young person is also more inclined towards growing up and meeting the world. Just before adolescence, he is apt to become rather restless and over-active — more difficult to reach and control. He may also express a preference for coarse language and vulgarity, and a disregard for order and cleanliness.

Arnold Gesell's description of the 13-year-old child gives a rather clear picture of the period of early adolescence:

> Thirteen is not always open and communicative. At home he may have periods of silence and musing. At school he is intensely interested, and shows a great capacity to absorb knowledge. At times he seems over-conscientious, and broods over many different worries. He is critical of his parents, and tends to withdraw from the family circle. The tendency to muse and worry are part of a process leading to self-insight and 'inwardising' awareness, which is one of the main features of early adolescence. But the child is also turning increasingly to the outside world. He is concerned with both inward and outward affairs. He is aware of his changing moods and tries to

think about them. He often seeks to be alone, whether in brief episodes or by taking long solitary walks.[8]

Boys as well as girls keep looking in the mirror to see what they look like, both to themselves and to others. This fosters self-discovery and awareness. But it may also cause pain and concern if the reflected image is disappointing. Even so, it may help to define a realistic sense of self. The world of real life, and also of stage, screen and literature, provides yet another reflecting mirror. In it the adolescent sees many different characters who have a strong influence on his growing self. He begins to feel some independence, and an inner resistance to his parents and others in authority. He is hungry for facts, and likes a teacher who can bring him knowledge.

During adolescence the child must gradually give up his early love for his parents, so that he may eventually find someone to love outside the family. His early love for them is not lost, but remains as a rich resource within him, which may appear in the form of religious feelings and ideals, and in the discovery of beauty and of a love for the world. The child now begins to contrast this inner world of ideals with the outer world in which he finds himself. If this world does not live up to his ideals, he may begin to rage against it. The discrepancy between these inner and outer lives is what gives rise to some of the turmoil of adolescence.

Adolescents need to be helped to find some sense and reason in the world order. Otherwise their inner turmoil becomes too great to control, or they become disillusioned and see existence as meaning-less. The adolescent wants to know the reason for everything and form his own opinions. He is no longer willing to accept everything on authority, and increasingly questions the values of his parents and teachers.

Young people today grow up with a view of the world in which everything can be explained in terms of sub-atomic particles. Inwardly, however, they cannot relate to this at all, because it has no human meaning. There is a growing uncertainty in the young — an emptiness and an anxiety, as if they dread the meaninglessness of the life opening up before them. They feel there must be some higher aim and purpose in life.

According to Rudolf Steiner[9], when the human being goes through puberty he brings his subjective nature (ego and astral body) into relationship with his objective nature (etheric body and physical body). (These terms are explained in Hans Heinrich Engel's chapter *Thoughts and experiences with adolescents.*) The search for a right relationship between subjective and objective gives rise to a kind of struggle, which is what accounts for the contradictions presented by children at this stage.

One of the features of adolescence, says Steiner, is a readiness to love, which does not at first show itself in a sexual form, but in a general sense of love for everything — a widened interest in people and events, and in the facts of the world. Young people begin to form friendships in which the friend is to some extent idealised. The friend seems to embody a quality which the young person would like to possess. At first most youngsters feel drawn to a friend of their own sex, and it is only later that they begin to admire and love someone of the opposite sex. Furthermore, says Steiner, the astral body is more significant in girls than in boys — more differentiated and organised. During her teens, a girl's ego is more under the influence of her astral body, and is gradually absorbed into it. In boys, the ego is not drawn into the astral body to the same extent; it remains hidden and is not properly active. Rudolf Steiner continues:

> One can often notice certain differences between adolescent girls and boys. Girls are often more at ease socially. They may have a bit of vanity, and value outer appearance and dress. Boys, on the other hand, often tend to draw back, and are more reserved and retiring, as if guarding some inner secret. They may show more need to withdraw into themselves, to be alone with their thoughts and feelings. If a boy does not show such reserve, it is a sign that something is wrong, which the teacher needs to look into.

> A kind of shyness takes hold of the child, arising from the perception of thoughts, feelings and ideals within him that he wants to keep secret and not reveal to the world. The outward behaviour is often entirely due to this shyness, despite the fact that it is so modified as to be turned into its exact opposite. Girls are often rather pert and

cheeky and stand on their dignity, while boys are typically awkward and surly. Much of the rough and rude behaviour of teenage boys arises from a desire not to show who they really are. The adolescent boy models himself on other people, but is reluctant to lay bare his real self before the world. He may therefore appear quite different from the person he really is. A sense of humour is needed when dealing with boys of this age. While enquiring thoroughly into any mischief or trouble that occurs, you should at the same time let each one see that you don't take his behaviour for the real person. You have to recognise this inner shyness and treat it with tact. [9]

Steiner also noted that a feeling for the beauty of nature, and impressions of a religious and moral kind, work against overt sexuality and eroticism. Eroticism involves being oppressed and tormented by one's body. Girls benefit from being shown the beauty of the moral and religious, and boys from the courage and power that comes from this.

Early adolescence

In early adolescence the child is struggling with a need to become independent of his parents. The passive role of being controlled must give way to an urge towards self-control. This conflict between active and passive, between independence and continuing dependence, becomes a crucial issue during adolescence. The more a child feels he is in a passive, dependent role — if, for instance, he is very protected — the more he will try to counteract this by means of rebellious feelings and actions. Such a child may complain that his parents do not give him enough freedom, even if in fact they wish him to be more independent. It is really his own fear of freedom that he is fighting against. The result may be a clinging and demanding teenager who is lacking in both initiative and interest.

During the early adolescent stage, boys go around with other boys in groups or gangs, which gives them a feeling of support and security. These groups form a halfway house between living in the family and living independently in the community. Girls, when anxious, are more able than boys to allow themselves to feel dependent on their parents, and so are less dependent on their own age group for support. They often go around in twos or threes. Friendship is important to girls of this age; they need someone to confide in.

Adolescents still need adults who are really interested in them and can also control their behaviour when necessary. But if adults are to carry any weight with an adolescent, they must be somebody whose authority he respects. A grown-up must become the youngster's hero if he is to have any influence on him.

Fantasy and creativity are at a peak in adolescence, which is a time for discovering the beauty of nature. Young people need opportunities to express the richness of their inner life in a creative and imaginative way. They have a longing to do something original, to bring something new into the world. Keeping a diary is a typical outlet for such feelings. Thoughts, events and feelings which cannot be shared with anyone else are confided to paper. The wartime diary of the young Anne Frank[10] is perhaps the best-known example of this.

Children who are late developers face special difficulties, often comparing themselves unfavourably with their friends. Boys especially may be teased for being smaller than their classmates, and may try to compensate for this by excelling intellectually, or by playing the fool, or being very assertive and rude. Their emotional growth tends to be delayed as well, further complicating the situation and calling for much sympathetic understanding.

Middle adolescence

The middle stage of adolescence often begins with a period of increased moodiness and defiance. According to Gesell[8], the 15-year-old is often indifferent or apathetic. He may be irritable and suspicious, perfectionist and self-critical. At home he tends to engage in a cold war. He comes in without a greeting, keeps to himself and resents his parents' restrictions. His spirit of independence is rising. He wants to cut loose and get away.

Away from home he is sociable and enjoys a crowd. He is involved in a conflict of attachment and detachment from his parents. He is more critically aware of their personality traits, yet he feels a growing anguish if they do not get on together. He suffers a real loss in having to give up his early love for his parents, and feels an inner emptiness, sadness and guilt (part of every mourning process) — hence his frequent moods of depression, apathy and withdrawal. Gradually, however, the inner turmoil and conflict diminish as he begins to become aware of his individual uniqueness. As he develops a firm feeling of his own identity, so he feels free enough of his parents to establish a new and more positive relationship with them.

From earliest childhood, children model themselves on their parents and other grown-ups. But during the mid-adolescent phase of identity formation, they have a particularly urgent need for people, real or imaginary, with whom to identify. They try out all kinds of roles and personalities in the search for a self. They look to the future, and wonder what they might become or what they might do with their life. This identification process is not always helpful, however, and children may pick up some of the worst qualities of their parents or other people. Youngsters in a borstal or approved school may easily become cold and harsh, and if anything even *more* confirmed in their anti-social tendencies.

If there are no helpful and significant adults in a young person's life, he will have no reliable or consistent backcloth to reflect his inner image of himself. As a result he will remain confused and unable to face the world, and may even withdraw into a psychotic condition. Alternatively, his feelings of emptiness and inner tension may lead to stealing, destructiveness and failure at school or work. This delinquent behaviour is really an unconscious attempt to provoke those around him to provide care and support, confirmation and recognition — in short, to mirror his identity back to him.

In boys, feelings of rivalry or rebellion against the father may lead to violent behaviour towards teachers or other people in authority. If a boy fails to do as well as expected at school, this may be a form of passive resistance against parental pressures to do well, or he may be afraid of competing with a successful father. In girls, delinquency usually takes the form of promiscuous behaviour or running away from home; this is usually a symptom of emotional immaturity caused by unhappiness or deprivation of love, or by other unfavourable experiences or relationships in childhood.

Erikson[11] describes adolescence as the stage of development in which the individual's main task is to establish a firm sense of identity. Adolescents are concerned with what they appear to be in the eyes of others, as compared with what they feel they are. The danger is that a youngster may become doubtful about his role or identity. Erikson feels that the stage of falling in love is not so much a sexual matter as an attempt to define one's identity by seeing it reflected in others and thus gradually made clearer. This, he says, is why so much young love expresses itself in or through conversation.

The adolescent is trying to find a connection between the richness of his inner world of feelings and ideals, and his outer life in the real world, which often seems dull, uninspired and trivial by comparison. If he can find no meaning or higher purpose in life, he may resort to delinquent or rebellious behaviour, or withdraw from everyday reality into a psychotic state. Failing this, he may build up a kind of false self in order to comply with the adult world. This means he has to compromise — repressing his ideals, and losing most of his young zeal, originality and initiative — and become an average conforming citizen. This may leave him with a feeling of deep dissatisfaction with himself — a feeling of incompleteness or lack of integrity. At this stage he needs support and guidance from adults who themselves have some faith in the ultimate meaning and purpose of life — who have not lost touch with their own youthful idealism, or at least have been able to rediscover it. Can you still remember your own adolescent contempt for everything bourgeois, trivial, dull or conventional?

Thankfully, by about 16 or 17 the identity crisis has been largely overcome, and the youngster has a sense of self that is reasonably realistic. His next task is to learn to cope with the complexities of life and try himself out. He is more sure of himself — more confident, stable and independent — and can therefore take criticism more easily. He becomes increasingly self-reliant, and develops a feeling of personal responsibility, for himself and for others too. This process can be encouraged by giving him the chance to feel useful in the community, and responsible for other people as far as he is able.

The extent to which a young person is able to become independent and self-reliant depends on how much security he has gained from his childhood relationships with his parents and other adults. If he is lacking in inner security, he may feel unable to face up to some demand or situation, and may revert to dependency on his parents. He may have to give up a job or course of study if it makes demands he is unable to meet. If a girl still feels the need to depend on someone and cannot turn to her parents for support, then she may easily rush into marriage. A lot then depends on whether her husband can fulfil the role of substitute parent and give her security.

Late adolescence and early adulthood

During late adolescence, the individual gains a clearer feeling for purpose in his life, and an awareness of what really matters to him. He may never put this into words, but it leads him to make certain choices which he feels are the only way he can be true to himself and find fulfilment, whatever struggles and hardships this may involve. What compels the individual to do this? If you examine a person's life history, you may often discern a certain ground tone: an element of continuity in spite of change; an underlying drive and direction. This may be due to a deep, semi-conscious awareness of his karma — his task in life — which begins to awaken during adolescence with the birth of the astral body.

Almost everyone has to cope with some handicap, problem or damage. This may arise from a person's constitution or karma, or it may have its origins in his childhood or environment. Gaining mastery over this pain and damage is an unending task in life. The person often seems to look for situations which repeat the original damage so that he can attempt to master it. Rudolf Steiner speaks of our unconscious will to do better in the future.

The young person now has to find ways of fulfilling life's tasks. At first he may go through a period of experimentation, in which he may seem to be aiming for many different goals at once. It is not always easy for him to leave this period of experimentation behind him and make a final choice — to finish sowing his wild oats and settle down. Instead of relying on his parents, he must now rely on himself.

A young person may sometimes enter a state of prolonged adolescence, in which he is unable to settle on any goal or task in life. Instead of trying to master situations himself, he seems to hope that circumstances will master them for him, and expects that his problems will be solved by luck or good fortune. He may feel that all would be well 'if only I had another job', or 'if only I lived somewhere else', or 'if only I were better-looking.'

If all goes well, however, the young person will start to accept adult values, and will discover that the parents he felt so ashamed of during adolescence aren't so bad after all. Now he can appreciate their good and bad points more objectively. Having emerged from his long search for identity, he can allow this identity to grow and expand. He can afford to be open and receptive. He is able to accept that the identity he struggled so hard for is nothing final and must still retain the possibility of growth. He can afford to give himself to other people in friendships and partnerships, and to commit himself to oneness with another person in marriage.

One possible danger at this stage is the kind of isolation that can result from a lack of openness towards new experiences or other people. Afraid of losing his identity, the young person may try to avoid situations which call for commitment or giving of himself to others. He may feel a need to keep people at a safe distance, and to reject any new idea or point of view. This gives rise to a narrow, rigid type of personality which, if it becomes extreme, may become subject to psychotic withdrawal and isolation.

There is, however, another kind of person who has difficulty in gaining a sense of identity. This is the affectionless or psychopathic personality. Such a condition may be due to a number of causes. The person may have been deprived of maternal affection, or may never have had the benefit of a father's guiding influence — or perhaps the discipline in his childhood was too lax, too severe or simply inconsistent.

The psychopathic person is always changing his mind, his mood, his way of dressing, or his job, as if in a desperate search for himself. He has a desperate need to be recognised as somebody, because he feels he is nobody. He has to provoke a reaction from the people around him in order to prove to himself that he exists — that he is real. Also, because he lacks a firm sense of identity, he is unable to form a mutual relationship with another person. He cannot trust anyone in case they let him down. He even seems to set out deliberately to prove this to himself by provoking rejection, or by shying off whenever someone begins to mean something to him.

Psychopathy is most obvious during the period of early adult life. Before this stage it is difficult to differentiate from the more extreme forms of adolescent crisis, and after the age of 28 to 30 it seems to burn itself out, leaving in its wake a rather empty, inadequate, petty, depressed kind of person.

* * * * *

There is of course a great deal more that should be known, and could be said, on the subject of adolescence. However, the few ideas explored above may help to stimulate further discussion and research.

Adolescence

Hans van der Stok

from a lecture given in Beaver Run, USA, January 1973

C arlo Pietzner once gave a vivid characterisation of the time in which we live.[12] He described it as a time of violence, aggression and anarchistic attitudes, and also (on a positive note) of sudden expressions of true human understanding, compassion and openness to the spirit. In short, he characterised it as a time of adolescence. John Steinbeck in his little book *America and Americans*[13] made a comment that is strongly reminiscent of Carlo Pietzner's description: 'The Americans, they are aggressive and defenceless.' This description also embodies something of the quality of adolescence, which again seems to link it to the time in which we live.

Given that this time of adolescence still holds us in its grip, perhaps the first question we should ask is when this time actually started. Perhaps the most convincing answer is that adolescence for mankind started in the Renaissance — a historic era of mighty geniuses, and of tremendous clashes between light and dark, not only outwardly but also in the human soul. It is the time when we also meet the dawn of freedom — the first attempts to break away from the powerful guardianship of state and church. The development of the printing press and other inventions opened the door to a world which allowed a person to judge for himself.

The Renaissance, therefore, marked the beginning, not only of the time of adolescence, but also of the search for freedom. The search for freedom by necessity leads to loneliness, because a person cannot become free without having been lonely. We could therefore say that at the present time humanity has truly arrived in the desert of loneliness — a loneliness that has become unbearable for many people. This may well account for the many acts of violence and aggression, and for the use of psychedelic drugs or similar attempts at escapism.

* * * * *

Having looked at some of the general background to adolescence, let us now turn to some of the more detailed aspects.

Rudolf Steiner in his series of fundamental lectures on education[14] describes the two poles which characterise every human being: the pole of *consciousness*, mainly centred in the head; and the pole of *will*, which is connected with the metabolic/limb system. When describing these two poles he speaks about *antipathy* and *sympathy*, but he uses these two expressions in a very unusual way — not in the customary moral sense, but in the sense of *non-involvement* and *involvement*.

Man in his will (the pole of sympathy, in which he is not conscious) is by necessity continuously involved with the world and with other human beings. At the other pole, where man is able to think and form concepts, there by necessity he cannot be involved, or else he would not be able to be conscious. He has to keep a distance from the world. He reflects, and even rejects, in order to be able to think. Thus Steiner uses the word antipathy for the conscious part, centred in our heads, and sympathy for the unconscious — i.e. the world of our will.

Now it could be said that in the nineteenth century, especially in the latter part, the perceived importance of the conscious — reflecting, rejecting, intellectual — reached its peak. However, at the beginning of the twentieth century new forces suddenly entered the world. For this was the time Rudolf Steiner gave spiritual science to the world. Spiritual science makes it possible for us to reach a higher level of consciousness in which the normal intellectual consciousness and the unconscious will may at last find mutual redemption. The same period saw the appearance of yet another new school of thought, namely psychoanalysis. This is an attempt to probe into the depths of the unconscious — though without fully understanding the nature of the forces that are revealed during analysis.

The third modern development that should be mentioned is no more than a concept, but it is one that has greatly contributed to the undermining of man's intellectual, conceptual life. This is the concept of relativism: the idea that we cannot know the absolute truth, and that all things are relative. Relativism has quickly taken over in the realm of thinking. Its undermining tendency reveals itself in the fact that it is not uncommon to meet people, even quite nice people, who will proclaim something with great conviction one day and something quite different the next day. This happens because thinking has become uncommitted. The human soul is no longer identified with the realm of thinking. Consequently, if you talk to black people in Africa, they may say, quite justifiably, 'You white people, we can't trust you. One day you think this, the next day something different. You are hypocritical. You don't believe in what you yourself proclaim.' Here is an example of how relativism can undermine our thinking. And what is the consequence? If our thoughts are no longer morally committed, how can we judge deeds or actions morally? We can't.

This moral relativism is yet another of the problems we face in the time of adolescence in which we live. It is understandable that under such circumstances people move away from the realm of uncommitted intellectual thinking towards the realm of what Steiner called sympathy. He used this word for the area of the unconscious will, and was fully aware that it presupposes the presence of destructive forces. Even if our actions and deeds are questionable, the forces through which we do them, and by which we involve ourselves, are basically the forces of sympathy, albeit misdirected. Thus people today often turn towards the pole of sympathy, but this often results in sympathy gone wild — sympathy without any guidance from the pole of consciousness — because they no longer trust their thinking.

The current climate inevitably influences young people. Today's adolescents are growing up in a world that bears the imprint of their own problems to a much greater extent than is normally realised. Parents and teachers are often as helpless as the adolescents themselves. They have lost the confidence and hope which perhaps their grandparents had. Two world wars, and many other things which I don't need to mention, have shaken their belief. Material and techno-logical progress, and the search for freedom, which by necessity has involved loneliness, have given way increasingly to fear and despair.

There is yet another aspect that further accentuates this highly critical situation. Rudolf Steiner repeatedly pointed out that mankind today is crossing the threshold. What did he mean by this? And how does this help us understand adolescents and teenagers today? Well, crossing the threshold means, among other things, that the boundary between the sensory world and the supersensory or spiritual world becomes vague. Unbeknown to us, the supersensory world starts to invade our daily lives. We have conscious or unconscious experiences which we are as yet unable to understand or discern.

Recent experience suggests that even the borderline between day and night is changing and becoming diffused. The night belongs to the spiritual world, because this is the world we enter when we fall asleep. It would seem that in some strange way this nocturnal world is invading our daytime world. This is probably one of the reasons why young people today are finding it increasingly difficult to sleep properly — to enter the night in the right way. Dr Karl König in two of his *St John's Lectures*[15] directed his attention specifically towards young people and their sleep problems. In the deepest sense, these difficulties mean that many young people no longer meet their angel during sleep. What they meet are the spectres and demons which we ourselves have created.

Crossing the threshold also means that the unconscious starts to invade the conscious realm of our lives. This, on top of everything else, means that adolescents today face an even more critical situation. The result of all this is increasing fear and anxiety. In my view, there has been no time in human history since the beginning of the Kali Yuga† when human souls have been so filled with anxiety. We can be sure that much of the violence we see today has its roots in nothing but fear.

* * * * *

---

† The Kali Yuga was the last of the four ages of the world distinguished in the post-Vedic traditions of ancient India. Beginning in 3101 BC, it was a period of increasing opacity to the supersensory world — hence the name Kali Yuga, or 'dark period'. According to Rudolf Steiner, this period came to an end in 1899.

Within this critical world situation an adolescent not only has to grow up but also has to *become himself*. I have stressed these apparently simple words deliberately. What does it mean — to become oneself? Those of us who are older may perhaps think that, despite the many obstacles, we have more or less managed to become ourselves. But have we really? When we look back over our lives, there is an important question that comes to mind. Considering all the various possibilities — all the latent potential — within our souls during our own adolescence, have they really been allowed to come to fruition? Or were they simply swamped by circumstances, education or other influences, so that our potential remained hidden? It is helpful to ask ourselves such a question, and to go on from there to ask the question of what it means to become oneself.

But first, let us approach this question of 'becoming' in a slightly different way, and start with the birth of the child, in the physical bodily sense. Let us assume that when a child is born he is received with love and attention, despite the fact that his soul is as yet unknown to those who love him. In most cases the soul of a newborn child is an unknown quantity for the parents. He is simply a little body whom they love and care for, and nothing else.

Then comes the birth of the soul, and this takes very much longer. It involves the whole process of communication, which begins as the baby starts to babble, and continues as he begins to express himself in his mother tongue. Growing more eloquent, the child starts to communicate his joys and sorrows. The birth of the soul lasts through all these stages of development, reaching its conclusion only at the end of primary-school age.

What, then, of the birth of the spiritual part of our lives? When does that happen? The answer to this question is found at the time of puberty and adolescence. The process that occurs then is all too familiar: a child who has hitherto been as open as any healthy child suddenly closes in on himself, like a book being shut, and puts on a mask. In my opinion, psychoanalysis has placed too much weight at this stage on the awakening of sexuality — though that admittedly also plays a part in the adoption of the mask. But there is another development which is far more important: something begins to stir within the child's soul, as if his soul were trying to give birth to its true spiritual self. At an unconscious level, the adolescent experiences this as something very tender, or even holy. It has to be nourished, but it also has to be protected from exposure — and this is why he adopts the mask.

How does this process continue? Well, this is the turning point that so often ends in terrible tragedy. In so many cases the adolescent seems to be unable to put the mask down again and give birth to the spiritual part of his being.

It may sometimes happen that you are able to be with someone who is passing over the threshold of death. Then suddenly, shortly before death, you may see that person's true individuality revealed — the individuality which was never able to break through during his lifetime. In some cases, then, the moment of spiritual birth coincides with that of physical death. This is a shattering thought, yet it is necessary that we learn to face it, because it touches on one of the deepest problems of adolescence. And this is not only a problem for adolescents themselves; it is one that concerns all of us.

What is actually meant by this spiritual part of our being that is waiting to be born? Many people are inclined to associate the spirit with the realm of what Rudolf Steiner called antipathy — the conscious pole of our existence. But if you want to gain a proper understanding of what is spiritual, then there is something else that you need to understand: the gifts which lie in the skilful fingers of a craftsman may be far more spiritual than the brains of a whole university. Once you have grasped this truth, you will have grown nearer to the reality of the spirit.

* * * * *

There is one question that must be answered in relation to adolescence. Why do young people turn increasingly against their parents and teachers, against society and the so-called establishment? I am convinced that this is because, although they are not consciously aware of it, they feel deprived of something which they expected to receive from their parents or teachers, namely the key to understanding their own problems — the key that could open the door towards their true selves. Because of this they feel deprived; and I dare say all adolescents and teenagers are more or less deprived children, not because they have been neglected by their parents, but because they have not been given the key to understanding their own and each other's true selves. That is where the problem lies. And because they feel deprived, they look for some way of compensating for this, such as drug abuse and other such things.

There is a most wonderful period just at the beginning of puberty when a young person may suddenly display some extraordinary talent or promising potential. If you observe carefully, you may often find highly gifted poets and mathematical geniuses amongst such young people. But this period of genius only lasts a short time before going underground and disappearing from view. You have the impression that something is trying to blossom and flower — the tentative expression of that spiritual part of the soul that is waiting to be born. Yet in the end it does not find the strength to achieve this. It is pushed underground, only to be followed by those typical expressions of a person imprisoned in his body. The young person now becomes revolutionary, antagonistic, because unconsciously he feels betrayed.

To seek a solution we must turn to what psychoanalysts call the unconscious, and what Rudolf Steiner calls the spiritual world. What do we meet at the threshold of this unconscious or spiritual world, where as adolescents we are meant to give birth to our true spiritual selves but are unable to do so? What is this world of the unconscious, and what do we meet there? In the sensory world we have learned to distinguish between, say, a tree and our own body. These are not so difficult for us to distinguish. However, when we stand at the threshold of the so-called unconscious, we meet spiritual forces, both angelic and demonic, which we have to learn to distinguish. And here our true self is to be found in a kind of enchanted state.

Forces exist which are by no means beneficial. Our present situation today contains an image that can also be found in innumerable fairy tales and myths — the image of a princess who is guarded by a dragon. You find it everywhere, and you can be sure that it is a true archetypal image, not just an arbitrary one. It expresses a reality that is to be found within the soul of every human being. The princess in all the fairy tales is the part of our soul which wants to give birth to our true self. The dragon is the other part of the unconscious that tries to prevent the princess from being liberated or even acknowledged.

The princess and the dragon is one of the most important images that can bring us to a deeper understanding of adolescence. Nobody can liberate my princess for me: I must do that myself. But we can learn to help each other in this process by acknowledging the reality of the image. *We have to learn to see the princess — the enchanted princess — in each other's soul, and especially in the soul of the adolescent.* We need to become spiritual midwives for each other. It is quite natural to fetch a doctor or midwife when a child is about to be born. But it doesn't occur to us that a spiritual midwife may be needed when a spiritual birth is due.

A learning process is required in order to become a spiritual midwife — to be able to recognise the princess in the soul of another person. As long as our souls are ruled by ordinary antipathy and sympathy, we cannot achieve this. We may think that sympathy for another person should be sufficient, but it is not. The adolescent, or the adult in a state of adolescence, will never be able to lift his mask and let us see his princess if we approach him with nothing but our natural sympathy. For what is natural sympathy? Natural sympathy is such that, albeit unconsciously, we always expect something in return. Natural sympathy is not selfless, and no matter how much of it we express to the other person, his mask cannot and will not be lifted, and the princess remains hidden. In other words, we have to overcome our primitive personal sympathy so that we can create a space where truly selfless love is present. Only then can we achieve entry into another person's holiest of holies.

This, then, is what is needed in order to become a spiritual midwife — to be able to help others through genuine recognition. If you achieve this, then you will have entered the inner space where Paul experienced his Damascus-road conversion — the space where John the Evangelist witnessed the cosmic vision that he described in Revelation 12: that of a woman clothed with the sun, with the stars above her head and the moon beneath her feet, in labour, giving birth to a child — and threatened by a dragon. Such is the greater, macrocosmic vision of the smaller, microcosmic image that lives within every human soul.

It is easy to understand why adolescents turn away from present-day society. But sometimes they go even further and turn against it. An understandable mistrust develops into a desire to destroy all forms of communal life. The deprived child becomes an anarchist — perhaps even a spiritual anarchist. But if a society is as sick as ours undoubtedly is, then it needs to be cured and not simply abandoned. The fundamental Christian principle of true (not sentimental) compassion is needed so that good will can be transformed into courage. True compassion, permeated by spiritual science, should enable the different generations to work together towards the creation of a new society worthy of the dignity of man.

The first necessity, however, is the true, selfless recognition of the princess in the soul of each fellow human being, and especially in the soul of the adolescent. If we prepare ourselves towards that end, then the time will come when mutual recognition is possible and the adolescent can start to recognise the princess in each of us. Unconsciously, the adolescent wants to know who we are. 'Who are you?' he seems to say to us because of what he feels deep down — that selfless mutual recognition is the only means of regaining hope and confidence in the future development of mankind.

> Only the help from man to man —
> the encounter of ego with ego —
> the awareness of the other man's individuality —
> without inquiring into his creed
> or his world concept
> or his political affiliations,
> but simply the meeting,
> eye to eye,
> of two individualities —
> only this creates the kind of curative education
> which may counter and heal the threat to the inner man.

> *Karl König*

The years in between

Rev. Michael Tapp

In: *The Threshing Floor* April 1981

In a recent report on crime in London, it was stated that more than half the offences were committed by young people under 21. This depressing statistic will probably be no surprise to any observer of our urban civilisation. Neither will it come as any surprise for those of us who for a long time have been gravely concerned, if not alarmed, at the onslaught of commercial interests on the fragile constitution of the teenage soul.

Unfortunately it is the young people themselves who are frequently blamed for this state of affairs, whereas in reality they are the innocent victims of our acquisitive and competitive society, whose values leave them open to every kind of unwelcome advance. The young people who resort to crime and violence are not doing so out of the natural character of their age group. On the contrary, such behaviour arises because their positive qualities as teenagers have little possibility of finding fulfilment.

Puberty is the biggest single change in the whole of our lives. The development of the physical organism and the achievement of sexual maturity are the outward signs of this change. During these years we see the gradual emergence of an adult physiognomy, as if an inner sculptor were moulding the external features that are to form the outer image of an indwelling personality. Never again, perhaps, until the closing moments of our life, will such radical transformations take place.

What is really going on behind these changes?

* * * * *

Looking back to the beginning of human history as it is related in the Old Testament, we read about the Creation, and about how on the sixth day man was brought into being. He was given a place in which to live, and in his original state of innocence everything was available for him to enjoy except the tree of the knowledge of good and evil.

The story that follows is a familiar one. Man was tempted by the serpent, the state of innocence was lost and harmony was destroyed. The woman was told that she would bear children in pain, and the man that he would spend his life in toil. But the Lord God admitted that 'man has become like one of us, knowing good and evil.'

The first sign of this knowledge was when Adam and Eve realised they were naked. We see the knowledge of good and evil linked to the awareness of being naked, and of those forces which reveal themselves in the differentiation of man from woman. It meant expulsion from paradise. The story continues: 'Now Adam knew Eve his wife, and she conceived and bore Cain.'

So the Fall of man brought us an awareness of our sexuality and the knowledge of good and evil. But it also brought more than this. The Fall marked the beginning of the endless 'wheel of becoming', and with it an intense longing to return to paradise. Buddha taught us that the working of karma — the law of cause and effect which chains human life to a constantly recurring material existence — can be overcome through the pursuit of the 'middle way' in the renunciation of all desire.

Applied in a purely physical sense, the law of cause and effect means that two human beings beget another human being, and that their offspring is moulded by his physical heredity and environment. Applied in a spiritual sense, it means that a human being brings with him into life all that has accrued to the human race and to him as an individual in the 'wheel of becoming', which has been turning since his expulsion from paradise. But during the course of human history, and after the time of Buddha, Christ also lived on the earth. This fact has to be seen as yet another cause, with its own effect on the 'wheel of becoming'.

This picture of the origins of human history suggests that puberty is intimately related to the original Fall. We leave the paradise of childhood and awaken to the forces which bring maturity. But these forces, like all the forces which man needs for his future evolution, are somewhat of a two-edged sword.

The Fall was not an unmitigated disaster. It may have brought a threat to man's existence, but it also gave him the chance to become a unique, free and creative being. The fact that we can face that threat with a certain confidence is something we owe to Christ. At puberty we enter into our inheritance, not only from the Fall, but also from the deed of Christ. This inheritance is personal in the sense that we each discover our own 'wheel of becoming' — our own bundle of cause and effect, which contains the mystery of our present life.

* * * * *

The Christian sacrament of confirmation can now be added to the picture.

In the teenage years we see how strongly human life is directed earthwards, towards the body and the world, and how the line that marks the relationship between the heavenly and the earthly is crossed. In his innocent state of childhood the young person has received the guidance of parents and teachers. But now he undergoes a transition: adult protection is gradually withdrawn and is replaced by the individual himself. During this time he awakens in a number of different ways.

Firstly, he awakens to his own independence, and becomes aware of himself as an individual with his own identity. Secondly, he awakens to the world as a wonderfully fascinating place to be explored and enjoyed. Thirdly, he discovers that both the world and himself (in that order) are imperfect. Lastly, and most importantly, he awakens to his own ideals, which are in stark contrast to what he finds in the world. The later teenage years should be filled with the urge to conquer the shortcomings of the world.

It is therefore imperative that the young soul should have access to the highest ideals, not only as ideas but as a gift of substance. To balance the Fall, and to strengthen the positive intentions which he experiences as ideals, he needs the grace of Christ's presence.

Sexuality and the knowledge of good and evil are presented to the young person today in tragically perverted forms. He needs boundless inner strength to live through this, and to receive into his soul the power of the One who can maintain and develop his delicate potential for the future. Through this he may in time come to see his ideals in the light of Christ himself, and to accept that the achievement of his own modest ideals will be a part of that same striving for resurrection which Christ achieved as the Ideal.

Christian confirmation cannot be expected to bring an immediate awareness of this. But it does implant a power in the human soul that will unfold with life itself, so that at each stage of life a person can find resources from within to meet the challenges that come from without. Confirmation is not intended to mark a Christian commitment or conversion, but rather to lay a foundation for the whole of life.

This means we should not entertain false hopes of young people joining the church. Our main concern should be not for their relationship to the spirit but for their relationship to the world. That is not to say that they should not come to church. But it does mean we need to accept that the world is where they belong, and that they cannot find real contact with spiritual communities until they have put strong roots down into the earth. To do otherwise might even be unhealthy.

* * * * *

In our teenage years we are neither children nor adults. The child bears something of the innocent origins of human history. The adult is fully immersed in working with, and through, mankind's fallen state. In between, there is an open situation in which the forces for the future are born, carrying with them a desire to change the world.

Thoughts and experiences with adolescents

Dr Hans Heinrich Engel

from a lecture given in Glencraig Community, Northern Ireland,
December 1966

In the first seven-year period of life, a child should experience that *the world is good.* In the second period up to the age of 14 or thereabouts, he should experience that *the world is beautifu*l. In the third seven-year period up to and around the age of 21, the young person should experience that *the world is true.*

Each of these three stages has its own starting point or birth, which opens up the possibility for achieving the experiences described above. These three births are:

Firstly, the birth of the physical body, when a child is born onto the earth.

Secondly, the birth of the etheric body, which gives the child entry to the elemental world that stands between the earth on the one hand and the human being on the other. It is the world in which is continually whispered 'The world is beautiful: look at it.'

Thirdly, the birth of the astral body: the moment when childhood ceases and puberty begins. At this point we are born a third time, and removed from the protective astral sheath or mantle of the mother. This is the moment when we are truly born into mankind — into manhood or womanhood. We must now experience our humanity, all that man creates, and all that is true as well as untrue, good as well as evil.

All of the above implies that people who are older bear a great responsibility towards anyone younger than themselves, and especially towards young people under the age of 21. Whenever we carry such responsibility towards a young person, there is one main question that we must keep asking of ourselves: 'Do I do live my life out of an experience of truth?'

The experience of truth should be available in us at any moment, so that the young person can sense its presence. This will become a factor in how young people are able to learn.

The first three seven-year periods of life can be likened to the phases represented by the first three post-Atlantean epochs: the Indian, the Persian and the Egyptian.

1   When we are born, like the ancient Indians we are not yet concerned with our physical body.

2   The situation changes after the second dentition. In ancient Persia, Zarathustra had to teach mankind to look to the world — to till the soil, to sow and reap. Similarly, as children we have to learn how to deal with the world.

3   The third period is associated with the Egyptian epoch — Babylonia, Chaldea and Assyria. Here we experience the world of the stars: the great stars, the planets and other large celestial bodies. During that period they were reflected directly into man's astral body. Man knew that the world was indeed true. So long as this was a direct experience, man knew the truth. When images of Osiris, Isis and the Horus child emerge, we can witness the imminent dawn of the birth of the ego.

Now let us consider the various faculties that can assist development in the various seven-year periods:

1   During the first seven years, the dominant faculty is the power of imitation — although this is something we never actually lose.

2   In the second seven years, authority plays a leading role.

3   The third period is characterised by the power of reason and the emergence of ideas.

1   Imitation helps to form a child's thinking. It also uses his

willpower, and should lead to an inner feeling of gratitude for what he has imitated.

2   When a child faces true authority — not the imposed authority that is usually implied by the term — his emotional life changes so that he is able to develop a natural affection for his fellow men and for the world.

3   In the third period the development of the will predominates. As you elect to do things for their own sake, so you recognise their inherent value and a sense of duty arises naturally from this.

These three periods culminate in the awakening of conscience, which shows that the ego has fully emerged and is beginning to play its part in the life of the individual.

* * * * *

The above presents an idealised formulation of the process of human development up to the age of 21. Human development is described in terms of three successive births: a physical, a sentient, and an intellectual, emotional or soul birth. These in turn are linked to earlier developments in human history, thus correlating the growth of consciousness in human culture with that in each individual person. Early childhood is linked to the ancient Indian civilisation, later childhood to the Persian, and adolescence to the Egyptian period.

The learning processes change as the child develops. He first learns through imitation, then through an authority figure such as a teacher, and thirdly in adolescence through the quest for truth. In response to these developments, certain attitudes arise naturally within the growing individual: firstly gratitude, which is related to the experience that *the world is good*; then love, which is related to the experience that *the world is beautiful*; and finally duty, which is related to the experience that *the world is true*.

These three steps run in parallel with the changes in physical appearance and the developmental stages undergone by the small child, the school-age child and the adolescent respectively. They are also related to the three forces that give rise to the physical body, the etheric body and the astral body or intellectual, emotional soul faculty, all of which together become a vessel to receive the self or ego which heralds the beginning of adult life.

Young people with learning difficulties

Young people with learning diffculties face particular problems as they take the final step into manhood or womanhood. For this is the stage when they come face to face with the shortcomings of their first 14 years of life.

There are some children who have not been able to develop their imitative powers effectively, and there are others who are totally lacking in this regard. Imitation is then replaced by various fixations, or by chaos and despair. Then there are some children who manage to get through the first seven years, but in the second phase are unable to accept authority.

At puberty, as these young people enter the third period of life, we have to learn to respect each one's individual shortcomings. The period from 15 to 18 is a very difficult one. The young people have yet to achieve an individual identity, yet they have already taken on the role of a young man or woman, and no longer see themselves as children. Not until they have bulldozed their way through this period can they appear as fully fledged individuals. This they usually achieve around the age of 21.

During adolescence, instead of expressing their individual identity, young people prefer to follow the crowd and form gangs. Their individuality is present, but remains submerged as they concentrate on finding their general identity as a man or as a woman. This is also a somewhat problematic period. Authority is no longer their chief guiding principle, although some kind of authority is needed throughout everyone's life.

During the latter part of adolescence, each individual should develop a sense of duty. One of the most important factors that shapes our morality is the ability to take on duties off one's own bat, and to assume responsibilities because they make sense. Can we expect the same of young people with special needs? Well, it may be difficult for them, but it is possible. At the time when a young person is developing his own insights, it is right to expect him to take on duties of his own. This process should start in the final years of schooling, and in a school for youngsters with special needs we have to adopt methods that are appropriate to the second as well as the third seven-year periods.

Learning and working

Two of the most important aspects of late adolescence are learning and working. Learning is a process whereby a goal is attained or a skill is acquired. Working means that something is created — comes into being — that was not there before. The adolescent must learn while working and work while learning. This double approach is needed because the young person is in a transitional state — neither a child nor an adult. He is in a delicately balanced situation where forces from the past reach into the future, while forces from the future reach back into the present. It is vital to understand the delicacy of the situation if you are going to help him discover his ego, develop his conscience and enter the realm of working life.

Learning can be achieved by means of skills training. Each student takes his time to learn how to create something, following the whole proceess from the first design through to the finished product. It does not matter whether he produces one article or 40, provided he is able to participate in every part of the process. He collects the various materials, acquires the necessary instruments and tools, brings in any additional items that are needed, and starts to work on the job. He learns to handle the thread, the cane, the leather, or whatever material may be involved, until the article finally takes shape.

Skills training must include every single part of the process, from the initial idea to the finished object. It is quite wrong to keep the student on just one stage of the process; he would quickly establish one tiny skill and use it hundreds of times without having any idea of what is being made and what the finished item looks like. This type of work is only suitable for fully trained adults — for them there is nothing wrong with division of labour, piece work or such like. But students have to learn everything from beginning to end. Training should involve both learning and working — mixing and interrelating these two aspects as much as possible. Work should have the quality of learning, while learning must have the quality of work.

Remembering and forgetting

Every day we balance our ability to remember against our tendency to forget. What are these two qualities? They are qualities of the soul, and they bring about a change of consciousness. A young person's consciousness is in no way fixed, and he is exposed to a host of soul activities which are far from being under his control. But in the third seven-year period he must start to gain control through his own will.

Closely related to the human will are those forces that we call desires, drives and instincts. They are among the forces that help us control our will. Instincts have more to do with the will in our physical body, drives with the will in our etheric body, and desires with the will as it affects our astral body. The young person's will takes on this threefold nature.

According to Rudolf Steiner[14] yet a fourth element is required to bring order, and that is motive. Motives are the forces that best enable a young person to control his own will, while instincts are the least effective in this. Training should create motives, which in turn lead to motivation. Skills training, because it goes all the way from design to finished product, is training for motivation. It therefore enables young people to take control of their will, and this is vital for the awakening of the ego.

I have explained how instincts, drives and desires are linked to learning and working. But what have these three to do with remembering and forgetting? Well, remembering and forgetting are activities of our will. To remember is to awaken to something, to forget is to go to sleep in order to avoid something.

There are students who are unable to forget, whether voluntarily nor involuntarily; they are compelled to remember everything. This means they are always awake; they don't even wake up to remember, or go to sleep to forget; everything is always present. Yet to become an ordinary mortal we have to learn to handle this business of waking up to what has to be remembered and going to sleep over what has to be forgotten.

According to Rudolf Steiner, this twofold process must become subject to our will, even if only at an unconscious level. In our unconscious minds at the very least, we must be able to remember and forget at will. Trying to remember is an activity of the will, and we can work consciously at it. In doing this we are preparing for the birth of the Horus child — the birth of the human ego, which happens at the age of 21. To prepare for the birth of the ego, whether or not a person has special needs, the will must be trained. Youngsters who always remember must learn how to forget, and those who always forget have to practise remembering.

Young people who forget everything need to be introduced to working processes in a different way from those who remember everything. The first group will have to concentrate more on the working aspect of the learning process; with the second group the learning aspect of the working process will need to be emphasised. You can start to do this before the youngsters reach 16.

Social awareness

Work experience is also vital to the development of social abilities, which need guidance in order to grow, to broaden out and to find appropriate outlets. Work experience allows young people to taste, to experience and to feel a shared responsibility towards the work which their team is involved in. Such experience is essential for them to develop and broaden their social awareness, and to adapt socially to new situations. Each individual has to learn to co-operate with the individuals on either side of him; each has to be able to form part of a social unit so that a work team can be created.

* * * * *

Any young person who is not yet quite himself, or whose mind has become befuddled with all the problems he faces in life, needs to learn that to achieve adulthood means accepting suffering, and one's own suffering in particular. If he has special needs or physical disadvantages, he must learn to accept them, to transform them and to use them in service to others. Whatever disabilities a young person has to deal with, they can be transformed and used for the good of mankind. The task during these formative years is to guide young people so that as adults they can each decide what they are going to do with their lives.

Because young adolescents feel a need to belong to a larger group, they should if possible be accommodated in large shared rooms for a year or two, and only then divided into smaller groups. At the stage of growing into manhood or womanhood, the experience of living together in larger numbers is most helpful.

If such shared accommodation is not available, then they should occasionally be taken camping for three to four days in a 12-person tent. The experience of humanity — either male humanity or female humanity — will enter their consciousness and remain there, perhaps even to the extent that they become fed up with it. This in turn provides a much-needed stimulus for their developing individuality. Such is the aim of the Scout movement, and youth hostelling is yet another good way of achieving this.

We have to find ways for young people to experience the suffering of mankind. They must gain experience of themselves in their physical body, in their etheric body and in their astral body.

So the task emerges — to lead each young person step by step, through the ocean of manhood or womanhood, towards the gradual emergence of the ego. As the years unfold, let us continue to think carefully about this task, and let us try to find better ways of helping young people with special needs in the particular circumstances that face them in the latter part of the twentieth century.

Training in Adolescence

The pre-village training centre

Rev. Julian Sleigh

from *The Cresset* vol. 10 no 4, 1964

The impulse of the Camphill Movement to establish communities for adults with special needs developed out of the work of the Camphill Schools for children. However, the adults in these communities require a fundamentally different approach from the children in the schools. A young adult is no longer a 'patient' in need of 'treatment' or a child in need of education. He now has to take up his destiny with as much responsibility and maturity as he can. The task for those helping him must be based upon a full respect for his individuality, however handicapped that person may be.

Such an understanding brings with it a vital new insight, namely that adults with special needs have to be treated in accordance with their age. So often they are talked down to like children, as though they were not expected to grow up. Yet how vital are those precious years which prepare a young person for adult life! They must be formative in a every way if he is to awaken to his potential and achieve the transition into adulthood. The period between leaving school and adult life — i.e. from about 17 to 21 — can be accompanied by a total change in a youngster's personality. He begins to see life in its vastness; he is challenged and attracted by it, but at the same time feels diffident, unprepared and unsure of himself. This is the period when work begins — when school and holidays recede into the past — when the young person first realises the need to support himself in life, and experiences that deep-seated urge to contribute to society.

Once a young person enters a community of adults (assuming

that he does), the life there will make considerable demands on him. Not only will he have to be ready to take part in work and production, but he will also be expected to take his share of responsibility for the life of the village community.† The inner strength and stability of the village cannot be provided just by those who have to exercise overall responsibility — the co-workers. Those with special needs must also play their part, or else the village would be little more than an elaborate institution. For this reason it is better for a young person not to enter a village until he is sufficiently mature and prepared. The case for this will be even clearer if you bear in mind that he may well spend the major part of his life in the village, growing older and perhaps even dying there.

Pre-village training is therefore needed in order to bridge the gap between school and working life. But this training should be more than just a 'rehearsal' for life. It need not be the same as the work that follows, just as college or university do not aim to imitate the career that is to come later. Neither should it be merely a prolongation of school — although there are a number of substantial advantages in having the training centre closely connected with a school, and perhaps even sharing the same grounds. This is what happened with the pre-village training centres at Glencraig, Northern Ireland and Cloister House, South Africa, which were created in the grounds of fully established schools for children with special needs. Much of what follows is based on experience gained at Cloister House.

Training

In such a training centre, the accent should not be on production but on actual training. Yet anything the trainees produce can be offered to the school. They can, for example, work the land and pass on the produce for the school to make use of. The same can apply to the output of the various craft-oriented training workshops such as the bakery, the weavery, the pottery, the maintenance workshop and so on. Even a laundry and a domestic training centre can provide a service to the units where the younger children live, and for these

---

† The village communities referred to are the working communities like that at Botton Village in North Yorkshire, England, which are different from the so-called village communities whose main purpose is to offer general care and support.

younger ones it is good to see their older fellows at work.

Another solution might be to combine the training centre with a village. In such cases, however, the village will eventually tend to dominate, and may perhaps even squeeze out the training. And then there is a real danger that the forms and standards of adult life may be imposed too soon on young people who are not yet really adults.

A young adult in a village must settle into a particular form of work, probably specialising in one specific part of a productive process. The trainee, on the other hand, should not specialise too soon. He should learn the craft he seems best fitted for, experiencing (and if possible acquiring) all the various skills involved. But he should have an opportunity to learn more than just one craft; he should take his share in household tasks, and also work on the land for a time. In this way he will experience something of the many-sidedness of life, and in the process may develop some of the interests which were stimulated during his years at school.

Trainees should be expected to work hard, but not necessarily for long hours. The time spent in the workshop or out in the fields should be intensive, and trainees should acquire the habit of sticking to their work. But there is no need to work a set number of hours in one particular workshop. The length of a working day or week should be determined by the work on hand rather than being made to conform to an arbitrary schedule. Then, when the project on hand is completed and there is some spare time available, a trainee can tackle another task such as helping another work team. The point is that the trainees should learn to value time and should not acquire a 'trade unionist' attitude. They should regard themselves as members of a lively working community, where what counts is their own individual contribution to the community as a whole, whether through their main work or in any other useful way.

In training it is essential to aim at a thorough standard of craftsmanship. The training should be therapeutic, but for the older adolescent it will only be therapeutic if he is taken seriously. The work must be real and in no way just 'occupational therapy' if the trainee is to benefit so that he can endeavour, of himself, to establish and develop his own personality. The craft itself can also have a therapeutic element, provided that it also has aesthetic and artistic value. Design is of paramount importance, and this calls for imagination and inventiveness on the part of the craft teacher. It is also an essential preparation for the productive economy of the village, which is based on quality of finish and good design. A highly repetitive operation with little inherent aesthetic or creative value will have a dulling effect on the mind of a young person with special needs. Besides which, the village could not hope to compete with an industrial factory in this type of work.

Production in a village must therefore be conceived quite differently from factory output. The different crafts must give scope for the varied qualities possessed by people with special needs, some of whom are naturally more sociable, while others are endowed with a more painstaking genius. Whatever the work, it must be such that each person can devote himself to it and pour his own personality into the product. Expression can then be given to moral and human qualities, and this will not only enhance the individual's own personality and quality of life, but will enable him to produce articles that have a special value in themselves. In a word, the article produced must be *personal*. Thus in a village workshop, while a certain amount of division of labour will be inevitable, the combined work of a team should cover all the processes required in making the article, and what leaves the workshop should be complete. As a preparation for this, the trainee should be given the opportunity to follow through all the elements of a productive process, and so gain a feeling for the wholeness of the work. He will probably specialise later on, but by then he will have a broader understanding of the work in hand.

Personal care

Training for productive work is only one aspect of the formative life of a pre-village training centre. There are many other elements that are just as vital.

The first of these is training in personal care. The ability to look after your appearance, to make your own bed and keep your things tidy, and a sense of dignity and appropriateness with regard to clothing and manners, are all vital elements of adult life. A young person must be tolerant and respect the freedom of other individuals as much as possible, but to do this he must first know how to use his own freedom, and recognise that this implies a code of behaviour that affects every detail of daily life. It may sound petty, but even the way you blow your nose can be irritating for those around you, and if you are conscious of this you can avoid causing irritation.

Changing into smarter clothes after a working day and before the evening meal is a most valuable habit — one which the trainees readily adopt, simply because they like it. The evening meal then belongs to the more social, cultural or recreational part of the day. It can provide the opportunity for a conversation about world events and problems, or about even deeper matters. Or perhaps a situation that might otherwise call for a reprimand can be resolved in a way which the young people accept with openness and goodwill.

If a village is to become a place where young people can find their freedom as adults, then the training centre must be geared towards preparing the young people for this. There is a consequent need to set high standards of behaviour requiring a considerable degree of self-discipline. This in turn places heavy demands on those responsible for guiding the training centre, who must demonstrate exemplary self-discipline in every sphere of life. The young people will be looking for a pattern on which to base their efforts towards acquiring an adult approach to life.

Generally speaking, the training centre will have more people living together than in a village household. It is seen not as a 'family' but as a small community where young people can experience all the elements of community living, face all the inherent challenges, and as far as possible overcome them. At a training centre, for example, loss of privileges where necessary is still appropriate as a means of discipline, whereas in a village it should fade out completely, being replaced by other means of guidance.

Adventure

The vigorous, demanding life of a training centre must contain yet another element — one that is particularly appropriate because it answers so many of the needs of young people in that transitional stage between school and adult life. This element is adventure.

Whereas adults in a village will probably settle into a steady rhythm of life, trainees on the contrary should be encouraged to seek adventure and thereby learn to relax and enjoy themselves. There should be plenty of opportunities for outdoor activities such as riding, mountain climbing and various excursions. Adventure can also be found in the realm of culture, whether in playing music or in tackling a play. Indeed, it can include any experience where young people have to grapple enthusiastically and creatively with some difficult challenge. They should not be encouraged to grow old too soon; such experiences are too precious to be missed.

It is just this stage of development that creates so many social problems among so-called normal adolescents. Here, as in many other areas, young people with special needs can demonstrate to their 'normal' contemporaries that life still holds much joy and excitement, even in this age of television. Indeed, the cultural and recreational life of a training centre can kindle a young person's initiative and love of activity. As it is based on community living, it can distract him from the many all-too-passive entertainments that are so prevalent these days.

If a training centre is situated next to a school, the trainees can join in some of the school staff activities. At Cloister House, for instance, the trainees frequently take part in the plays performed by school staff for the children on festive occasions; they are also invited to attend lectures and artistic activities. Conversely, the school staff join in the regular folk-dance evenings at the Cloister House training centre, and this also gives trainees the opportunity to act as hosts.

As regards sports, it is good if a trainee can develop enough skill at one or two games so as to be able to take part. Not only football but the more individual sports should be encouraged, such as archery, javelin throwing, bowls, clock golf, putting, badminton, tennis, quoits, deck quoits or croquet. None of them require more than a flat lawn or a piece of paving, and little equipment besides. Such sports can also be helpful for young people with problems stemming from the fact that they are, for instance, not clearly right- or left-handed. While it is good to teach the young trainees in these sports, the emphasis should be social and not instructional, with the aim of stimulating their enthusiasm and sense of fun. Before they move on to an adult situation, it is important for them to develop a certain amount of initiative and independence in the area of sports and entertainment.

Education

Schooling should not be a feature of the training centre, but a certain amount of educational work can be woven into the programme. The period after supper is good for this, and small groups of trainees can be helped to develop their reading and writing abilities. For those who can read, it is vital for them to be encouraged to do so, but not just in a mechanical fashion. In Cloister House, for example, trainees who can read have regular sessions during the week when they read something of their own choice. When they have read a certain amount (each working on his own), they write a description of the contents in their own words with a view to preparing a short 'talk' on the subject. When one of them is ready, he gives the talk to the whole house community at the end of an evening meal after the tables have been cleared. These talks often stimulate interesting discussions, while the young people themselves gradually improve their ability to express themselves. This encourages them, not only in their reading and writing skills, but in their openness to the world in general.

Spiritual life

There is one final aspect to be considered, and that is the spiritual life of a training centre. There is much that could be said and discussed on this subject, because it is the vital formative influence that can awaken the personality of a young person with special needs, deepening his awareness and giving him a sense of being able to share fully in the dignity of mankind despite his difficulties. One evening a week is devoted to spiritual studies, and the trainees gather for prayer at the beginning and the end of each working day. All this, together with preparations for Sunday and the various festivals, is something that everyone can take part in and gain something from.

The weekly study is not a lesson but a social occasion, attended by all the co-workers as well as the trainees. Thus it is very much part of the fabric of life, which is open for everyone to share. The Sunday service is the focal point of the week. The efforts to learn and train, to develop and produce, to become more responsible and more socially minded — all the adventures, disappointments and failures of the week — all fall into perspective when taken and offered up at the altar on a Sunday morning. The transformation of raw materials, the striving for beauty and aesthetic experience, the tilling of soil teeming with nature in all its abundance, and all the joys and challenges of sharing in the communal life, are all part of leading a purposeful Christian existence. They can be offered up as the bread and wine of life, awaiting its ennoblement, its transformation and its true end, which can only come through the Spirit.

* * * * *

Thanks to all these elements of training, young men and women with special needs can prepare themselves for a full and useful life as members of a village community. Problems and difficulties can recede in importance, and the intact personality living within each one of them can flow into the life of the village community and out into the world at large, which longs for those personal qualities that can provide a balm to soothe the spiritual suffering of our time.

Training and further education
of adolescents with learning difficulties

Dr Hans Heinrich Engel

from *The Cresset* vol. 13 no 2, 1967

A round the 14th year, the child moves into the third seven-year period of his life. This transition entirely alters the child's outlook on the world. He now feels the need to enter into a completely new relationship with the world, and into a similarly new relationship with himself — or herself, as the case may be.

Up to this age the child has usually been willing to accept his status as a child, and the consequent need for guidance and education from his parents and other adults. But as soon as puberty begins to take effect, something new starts to happen. He discovers emotions and feelings that give him a new sense of his own independence, and he starts to react differently to various stimuli. Up to now he has tolerated the authority of a teacher or superior, sometimes even to the extent of liking it, but from now on this becomes a burden and an impediment to his searching spirit. As the adolescent starts to look at the world around him, so he lights upon some other, more attractive personality. He then redirects his inner feelings and emotions towards this person, who becomes the object of his new-found loyalty. Nowadays the most likely choice might be some well-known personality in the field of sport, film or some other form of popular entertainment. Or it might be a more tradi-tional figure such as a famous military leader or explorer, a scientist, dramatist or poet — or perhaps even some great humanitarian. The young person creates his own ideal — or maybe even idol — and shares his new-found enthusiasm with other people.

At this stage the youngster's feelings become strangely polarised. There is one part of him that feels on top of the world: no goal is beyond his reach, and he still thinks he can be a master without having been an apprentice. Yet there is another part of him that feels increasingly tied down by the demands of the world, not just in the area of work but also within his body and soul. He turns to his friends and peers to find out what their situation is; this helps, but at the same time it disturbs him.

This process goes through various stages during the seven years leading up to a person's 21st birthday. Indeed, each year is like an instrument tuned to a different key, and sounds accordingly. Around the seventeenth year, these developments reach a kind of climax that is also a turning point, carrying within it the seeds of change.

The most important development during this period is the young person's awakening to the fact that he or she is no longer a child and is taking on part of the destiny of mankind by assuming the state of manhood or womanhood. The onset of puberty is sometimes likened to that moment after the Fall when Adam and Eve discovered that they were naked, and it is from this point onwards that male and female each begin to develop in their own specific ways. This is how Rudolf Steiner describes the different spiritual changes experienced by girls and boys during puberty:

> Until now his place in mankind has permitted him to imitate, to accept authority. Mankind worked upon him from without, whereas everything within him resulted from what he had brought with him from his pre-existence. Mankind as an entity first influenced him in the way that he imitated it, and then by his being under its authority. Because he has found his own way to mankind, his soul now acquires a certain sensitivity — a feeling for the general existence of humanity — and this becomes the counterbalance to his newly developed powers of procreation. Physically he becomes capable of propagating; spiritually he is able to experience the whole of mankind within his soul.[16]

These experiences within the young person's soul will differ according to whether that person is male or female. For the young woman, mankind appears more in the character of an image — as a gift bestowed on her. The young man, however, experiences mankind more in the form of a riddle. The process of solving that riddle arouses his longing and desire, and this influences him as he begins to shape his relationships with the opposite sex.

During these years, however, the young person is not yet ready to develop or grow into his or her own individuality; it is more a question of being taken over by a general state of manhood or womanhood. This is what causes young people to develop those aspects of youth that are so disturbing to the older generation. They succumb to the herd instinct and form groups or gangs; they formulate their own language, dress according to particular trends and fashions, and harbour thoughts of resistance, withdrawal and radical change. All this, and more, is in itself natural — even necessary — and was also acceptable so long as these groups or gangs were of a local nature, confined to a district, or a town or village. Now, thanks to our modern mass media, all this has changed; what is more, commercial interests have recognised this stage of psychological development in the young, and are happy to exploit it. Thus the passage through adolescence has lost its relative innocence and has become a problem all over the world.

This is the state the adolescent finds himself in at a time when he has to prepare for school-leaving examinations, university entrance, or training in skilled work or some other professional activity. It is a period full of turmoil and excitement, pain and resentment, high hopes and unfulfilled promises, until the day comes when maturity permits the development of individuality, and adult life can begin.

* * * * *

What do we find when we turn to the child with special needs? Is he also involved and engaged in these general problems of mankind? There is no doubt that he too passes through these phases of adolescence, although they may manifest themselves differently. Not only are there the obvious physical changes, but the changes are equally marked in the realm of feeling, sentiment and affection. There are Down's syndrome boys who will clearly choose someone to idolise, whom they will then imitate in every gesture and manner; they will even contradict their usual behaviour by undertaking to do something as a special favour for their 'idol'. Then there is the solitary autistic boy or girl who will always see to it that he or she is not left out, though such children will of course never openly admit to this. Even the choice of clothing reveals a strong urge to conform

For the so-called 'normal' child, the period of adolescence becomes increasingly a time of intensive study — of further schooling — requiring large amounts of facts and information to be absorbed. For the child with learning difficulties, however, the teacher will need to adopt a different approach. Such a youngster will ask for more and more guidance in finding out about the world — for a widening of his horizons. As this cannot be achieved by means of textbooks or abstract learning of facts, it has to be attempted by means of carefully prepared practical introductions to subjects such as physics, chemistry, geology etc. Learning has to be clearly founded in the life-situation of the child, and in the facts and events known to him through daily experience. This method can achieve astonishing results, enabling such children to understand the fundamental principles of organic chemistry, astronomy and other subjects. Through this process these young people become prepared to face the world; their powers of attention are increased, and they begin to relate in a different way to the world at large.

This is therefore the best age for fostering one of the fundamental aspects of human activity — namely *learning*. This activity is practised by everyone, and is something that should continue throughout our lives.

At the same time, however, there is a second aspect of human activity that is undergoing a metamorphosis. This is the activity that the child has so far experienced in the form of *play*. For the child, learning and play have formed the basis of his life, and now this play has to be transformed into *work*. Work should in fact emerge out of play. Continued learning should improve the young person's working capacity, while training in work activities should improve his learning capacity. The twofold combination of learning and training forms the basis upon which the training school can be built.

* * * * *

The way in which we apply these ideas in practice works as follows. Children continue formal schooling, usually up until their sixteenth year, but often for longer. The training school is the goal that most of them aspire to, and they concentrate their efforts, both at home and at school, towards gaining admission — and as this is a privilege and not a foregone conclusion, these young people may become anxious as the time approaches for taking this step. They will often have already decided for themselves which craft they would like to learn, and may even have decided whether they want to stay on afterwards in the surrounding adult community, or whether they prefer to leave after the two- or three-year training period.

On entering the training school, the new trainees will also become part of a house community where there are older trainees, house-parents and other adults. The trainees will have to take responsibility for looking after themselves, their own affairs, their rooms, the house etc. So a great deal of preparation towards this must be undertaken during the later years of schooling. If they are slow learners in these areas, then special efforts have to be made. The trainees will also have to do the cooking, albeit under the guidance of an adult. This in turn is linked to a domestic training course, the purpose of which is to equip the youngsters for independence in later life.

All matters to do with daily life are discussed by the house community as a whole. This is often a difficult process, requiring a great deal of ingenuity and patience on the part of all concerned. But it is amazing to see how quickly the trainees start to become interested in taking responsibility, and how keen they are to follow what has been agreed on the basis of these communal discussions. There is, of course, a great difference between a fresh school-leaver and someone who has already spent some time in the training school. Thus a natural division occurs between the beginners and the more advanced trainees. The grouping may change over the years as beginners move on into the advanced group. But the timing of this will vary, and some trainees may even stay on with the beginners for a period of several years.

The life of the house is interlinked with the programme of learning and work. The beginners' group continues for about a year with formal schooling in the morning. This is designed to serve two purposes: firstly to increase their knowledge of the world, and secondly to build on their sometimes modest achievements in the area of the three R's. The afternoon, however, is entirely given over to developing their skills in a training workshop.

This skill training, as it is called, is pursued according to a very specific programme. The new trainee is presented with one particular craft such as basketmaking, weaving, leatherwork, pottery or whatever, and he is introduced to the whole process, starting with the design and working through each individual stage until the product is finished and sold. It is essential that each trainee should accomplish every single step from the original design to the finished article. Productivity is not especially important at this stage; what *is* important is to complete the whole step-by-step procedure, because this method is vital to the training process as a whole. With the first craft it normally takes rather longer to achieve what is wanted, but perseverance eventually pays off. The process may sometimes take as little as a few weeks, whereas at other times it may last a few months.

When a group has completed skill training in a particular craft, it then takes up another craft. The same process is repeated and a new set of skills is acquired. The hard work devoted to the previous craft will soon bear tangible fruit, because the whole process is much faster this time. The sense of having improved encourages the trainees, who become happy and enthusiastic to achieve more: the workshop takes on an atmosphere of eager anticipation. In this way a number of skills are acquired, which are not superficial but firmly established.

The advanced group follows a different timetable. The mornings are spent in further skill training, similar to that described above. But in the afternoons the trainees go to work in the various workshops in the adult community. Here the prevailing attitude is quite different from that found in the training workshops. The primary emphasis is no longer on training but on production. Any trainee who is sufficiently advanced can now show how skilled he has actually become, and can apply his skills to whatever work process he has to do.

There is a very moving example that demonstrates what can be achieved by this training method. One young man, when he started skill training, was unable even to hold a needle because his vision was impaired and he had motor disturbances. However, thorough training provided him with a variety of skills, so that he was eventually able to handle various types of machine in the print shop, even though the techniques involved required accurate manipulation and good eyesight.

To sum up, then, the main emphasis during these years of training is on acquiring a large number of skills by means of a thorough grounding in the various work processes. At this stage production is only a side issue, albeit a welcome one. In working life, however, production begins to matter, even if it is then achieved by division of labour. Adult working life requires a maturity that can only be achieved through a period of training, during which the working processes are carefully worked through and completed under full supervision. In this way, through learning, play can be transformed into the acquisition of skills, and can then become true work.

Apart from skill training, continued schooling and the introduction into workshop life, there is a great deal more that the trainee has to experience. One day a week is set aside for background learning, which furnishes everyone with detailed knowledge about the crafts, factories and installations that provide the material basis for our way of life. Formal lessons are complemented by visits to factories such as rope works, linen mills, shipyards, synthetic-fibre manufacturers and others.

The trainees will also deal with the many urgent and important problems that beset the progress of mankind, and which ultimately affect the whole of humanity. These include disease, starvation, poverty, natural disasters, racial problems in different parts of the world, and the consequences of wars. The young person has to appreciate that he is an integral part of the body of mankind. His aspirations to change the world, borne from his revolutionary spirit, must be channelled into a thorough maturing process that brings him face to face with the problems and with the attempts to solve them. This enables him to become aware of his own standing — his own destiny — in relation to the destiny of his nation, or even of the whole of mankind. Thus the general state of manhood or womanhood can be gradually forged into the young person's individual experience. This process helps him to develop his own conscience, and awakens a feeling of social obligation.

The course also incorporates other more artistic pursuits such as eurythmy, painting, modelling and music. These not only provide recreation but also — perhaps more important — help to stimulate creativity. Other essential experiences include outside activities such as mountain walks, or trips to cities and to museums, theatres and concert halls, which also help the young people to gain more understanding of the world at large.

There are various programmes of evening activities. The youngsters are helped and encouraged to mend and maintain their clothing; they are always given sufficient space for initiative and creativity. Other pursuits include games, folk dancing, discussions, religious studies, walks, music and various hobbies. Some young people take up a musical instrument, while others are more interested in books. Plays are rehearsed for performance at the various festivals that take place during the year.

During the period when the individual is first experiencing the state of belonging to mankind, he may easily become bored, especially since he is unable to engage himself, and still needs the uniformity and conformity of groups. Yet he still needs to experience the greatness, the breadth and the beauty of the world and mankind, while at the same time recognising the suffering, pain and toil of human existence. Man's earthly life stretches from birth to death, between learning and working — and the growing adolescent has to discover and recognise this. It is just such an awareness which will give him the conscience and the strength of responsibility that alone can support his individuality — his ego — on the quest that is adult life.

Three Essays on Adolescence

Dr Karl König

Educating adolescents with learning or behavioural difficulties

from *The Superintendent's Report of the*
Camphill Rudolf Steiner Schools 1955

The age of puberty — the change-over from childhood to youth — is extremely important for the development of every human being, because it is the period when their individual personality starts to make its presence known. The individuality appears for the first time and starts to 'resound' (Latin *personare*) through the layers of the human frame. This great event is always observable in ordinary children, but in children with special needs, whether through learning or behavioural difficulties, it is a particular crucial period that is often characterised by a good deal of pain and sorrow.

The pain comes from the discovery that, despite all the help and care such a person has already received, his individuality has not become strong enough to challenge (and eventually conquer) the body's increasing weight and physical strength. As the body grows in size and strength, so the dim light of the individual personality can become overwhelmed, fading away almost as soon as it appears; then the adolescent boy or girl cannot unfold as a spiritual entity. Some young people may even revert, becoming dull, self-concerned and indifferent to the world around them.

The speed of pubertal change varies between different types of children. In one child it might be over within a few months, while in another it can take years. If puberty lasts a long time, then it is especially important (and effective) to provide some form of educational and curative activity. Puberty becomes a prolonged battle as those standing close by help to defend the young person's individuality. This sometimes means that the personality can be saved, thus securing the individual's whole future. However, if puberty sets in very quickly, then the battle is lost almost before it can start, and there is little scope remaining for providing any effective help.

In particular, I have observed that this quick change often occurs in children suffering from post-encephalitic and epileptic conditions. Within a few months a child can turn into a heavy, dull, immobile adolescent, who may even have to be discharged because little more can be done for him. Some pre-psychotic children have similarly undergone a sudden change at puberty, turning into severely schizophrenic personalities. Here again the battle has been lost, and they have sometimes had to be transferred to psychiatric hospitals. However, there are many such cases where the onset of puberty is slow, enabling them to be helped. The years between 13 and 16 years are so vital to a young person's development.

Boys and girls with behavioural difficulties present their own very special problems. Many of them are like strangers to the earth. Their family ties are loosened or broken, their bonds with other human beings are hardly established, and they have an innate will towards self-destruction. They look for trouble in order to destroy themselves, seeming to want death instead of life. Most of them are disappointed with life to the very core of their being. They are disillusioned and heartbroken, and during puberty all these symptoms become especially pronounced.

As long as they are still children it is enough to love them, but when they become adolescents they need more than just love. Is there anything greater than love? There is nothing greater, perhaps, but of greater importance to adolescents is their teacher's faith and self-control. Many of these boys and girls are very observant of their surroundings: they know whether an adult is speaking the truth or not; whether or not he believes in what he is saying; whether he is better able to control his emotions than his pupils. This is the main issue for the adolescent with behavioural difficulties in the fight between good and evil. Is the teacher willing to devote himself totally? — not 90 per cent, nor 98 per cent, but 100 per cent. If a teacher can do this without any trace of self-pity while maintaining his full self-respect, then the adolescent will respond. His disappointment will gradually be dissolved, and he will start to believe in the honesty of other people.

The teacher is the one person who can alter the child by altering himself, by continuous inner striving. If he speaks of God, the adolescent knows whether or not he means it; it is no use merely paying lip-service. When a teacher leads the Sunday service, the adolescent will test him throughout the week to see whether his words from the altar are carried through into his daily life. If they are, then the youngster can be gradually healed — he will learn to listen, and will do so with tremendous relief. At last he will have found the guidance and certainty that he strove for in vain throughout his childhood.

The healing power of the teacher's personality is not enough without the right eductional support, such as can be provided within the upper-school curriculum of the Waldorf Schools. Adolescent boys and girls have an urge to learn and a desire to understand life, provided that it is presented to them in a way they can accept. They do not want to know the scientific side of things; they want to understand the spiritual background of nature and man. If you teach them the history of art, you need to do it in such a way that they can see the path of the human soul throughout the ages; this will satisfy them. They need to learn science as it relates to human beings. If the fabric of the human body is presented to them in wondrous beauty, the effect can be miraculous, helping them to gain confidence in a life which they have so far only wanted to destroy. In this way each one's individuality will be helped to gain control over the power of the body, and a young person will gradually emerge who is willing to go through life in an ordered way.

For those adolescents with special needs who are blessed with a gradual onset of puberty, the problems are on a different scale. They are less in need of their teacher's example and guidance than of a constant source of stimulation. They need to have activity around them and to find ideals within their own souls. Their daily routine should be ordered with great care and attention, and they have to be continuously occupied in work. Their hands should never be idle, and their senses should be kept active, with as many fresh new impressions as possible. Periodic visits to concerts and plays, outings to factories and places of interest, hiking and camping holidays — all these activities are of importance. They need as much schooling as youngsters with behavioural difficulties, but they need more coaching and more individual work, because the foremost task is for the awakening personality to be constantly stimulated.

Puberty in all these adolescents is like an illness. If it occurs in an 'acute' form, little help can be given. In its 'chronic' form, however, the 'patient' has to be carefully observed and continually 'treated'. Curative education has a most important part to play here, because it is during these crucial years that the future life of an individual can be either won or lost.

The problem of delinquency

An indication by Rudolf Steiner

from *The Cresset* vol. 3 no 2, 1956

In recent times the problem of juvenile delinquency has been the subject of increasing public attention. It took on an even greater urgency in the early 1950s when investigators in the United States discovered that almost 60 percent of all crimes committed each year, including murder and manslaughter, were committed by young people under the age of 18. In January 1955, the then United States president, Dwight Eisenhower, asked Congress in Washington to grant a sum of $3 million towards the control of juvenile delinquency, thus showing that the public conscience could no longer be ignored.

This burning question became the subject of international conferences, including a major congress held in Geneva in 1955 and attended by leading psychologists and social workers from all over the world. Sadly, it ended in bitter disappointment. Each lecturer proffered his own special prescription, and the ensuing discussions became long-winded, fruitless and increasingly confused; delegates repeatedly came to the conclusion that the entire structure of our social order would have to be altered in order to stop the massive increase in juvenile delinquency. Such fundamental reforms were clearly impossible and we were left with a mere patchwork of auxiliary measures.

Around the same time, a sensational book appeared in Britain called *1,000,000 Delinquents* [17], written by Benjamin Fine, one of the editors of the *New York Times*. This book presented the tragic and gigantic dimensions of this problem. It was a kind of *Mene Tekel* written on the walls of our age, lighting up with increasing intensity.

Yet only a few people have approached these problems from the right point of view. Too much emphasis has been placed, for instance, upon physical processes — the idea that certain disturbances in the structure of the brain cause inherent 'criminal tendencies'. Numerous psychological and pseudo-psychological explanations have been sought. Reasons given have included the break-up of the family unit, the loss of maternal instinct in mothers, and the parents' incapacity for love. René A. Spitz, a well-known New York psychoanalyst occupied mainly with the mind and soul of the newborn child and infant, made his own contribution towards the delinquency problem by stating that the infant deprived of his mother's love 'grows up into hatred'.

Each of these conjectures, explanations, statements, contains a grain of truth. But we can never penetrate to the spiritual background of this problem unless we regard man as a being who has his roots not only in heredity and the collective unconscious, but in an individual past springing from the ground that lies beyond the threshold of birth. The real question is this: is there a common prenatal cause that forms the basis of all criminal tendencies? Does something happen during the time through which the soul lives between death and rebirth that manifests itself on earth as criminal inclination?

* * * * *

At the beginning of 1914, just before the outbreak of the First World War, Rudolf Steiner addressed this problem in some of his public lectures. In the January of that year, he spoke in Berlin on *Evil in the Light of Spiritual Knowledge*. The following March, also in Berlin, he addressed the theme of *Between Man's Death and Rebirth*, which he later repeated in somewhat altered form in Vienna (in one of a series of lectures) under the title *What can Spiritual Science say about Life, Death and the Immortality of the Human Soul?*

In these last two lectures, Rudolf Steiner dealt specifically with the prenatal causes of criminal predisposition. In Vienna he stated:

> When the criminal is observed clairvoyantly, it becomes apparent that criminal personalities are the result of a kind of spiritual

premature birth. Every soul has the potential to enter the physical world at its own appropriate time. But this tendency may be counteracted by other tendencies, with the result that some people — but especially criminals — arrive on earth much sooner than they normally should. This has several implications. The soul must enter the physical world around its normal time if it is to permeate the entirety of the physical body so that the human being can stand complete. If special circumstances arising during previous earth lives cause the soul to arrive on earth sooner than is appropriate, then something enters imperceptibly into the unconscious which can be described as 'not taking life seriously'. This happens because the soul has arrived at a time when it cannot connect fully with life on earth. The soul adopts a fundamental mood of 'not taking life seriously'. In ordinary consciousness there is a strong instinct for self-preservation, which in the criminally disposed can develop into the starkest egotism; yet at the same time the unconscious mind tends to take things at face value — to take things too easy — and is unable to value life because of a spiritually premature birth. However, as the soul passes through many lives on earth, this is levelled out again. Thus the criminal makes up in other lives for what he has done in that life to which he was prematurely born.[18]

Thus Rudolf Steiner points to spiritual factors leading to criminal behaviour. Criminal souls are those who did not remain long enough in the spiritual world before returning to the physical world to take up a new life. Metaphorically speaking, one might say that the bread of these souls was not thoroughly enough baked in the spiritual world before being offered back to earth; the baking process was hurried and incomplete.

Here the roots of today's delinquency are exposed. Life is no longer taken seriously, and is no longer felt to be a task that has to be mastered. The saying in the Bible that bread must be eaten 'by the sweat of thy brow' was never intended to refer to physical labour alone. It meant that the 'bread of destiny' offered to us by life itself must be eaten up completely, be it bitter or sweet. This, however, is no longer true of the experience of the millions of young people of today.

Countless numbers of modern young people behave like souls born prematurely, entering an earthly life for which they have been insufficiently prepared during the life between death and rebirth. To describe the situation more correctly, one should say that these human beings have remained too spiritual: they have brought with them too many spiritual qualities, and therefore remain estranged from the earth. The bread of their existence has not got enough crust on it, and for this reason life can only offer them fear, pain and vulnerability. The keynote of their existence is a predominant feeling of disappointment. Everything disappoints them because they are unable to find anything that might bring fulfilment and contentment into life.

There is no medical or psychological remedy for this condition. No drug, no amount of psychoanalytical treatment, can help in such cases. Improvement is only achievable if other people endeavour to create a common social setting and to implant a new seed by giving these young people a renewed confidence in the spiritual dimension. To take but one example, the youth of today must learn to recognise the necessity and the true value of earthly life.

To fall into sin and to rise above it must not be seen as a single, once-and-for-all event, but as one that recurs over and over again. In the New Testament, the apostle Paul says something rather interesting when speaking of himself as one of those who has seen the risen Christ:

> And last of all He was seen of me also, as of one born out of due time. For I am the least of the apostles, that am not meet to be called an apostle, because I persecuted the Church of God. [I *Corinthians* 15: verses 8–9]

Perhaps this is yet another example of a premature birth. Perhaps Saul, as he was originally called, was born prematurely so that he became a persecutor of Christians. It was only after his experience on the road to Damascus that he was able to cast off his Saul identity and assume that of Paul. It would seem that in today's world there are vast multitudes of Saul's companions waiting to become companions of Paul. This is something worth considering, perhaps, for everyone who hears the voice of conscience today.

Alarming symptoms in the physical and mental development of our youth†

from *The Cresset* vol. 3 no 3, 1957

In the mid-1950s scientists drew attention to a phenomenon that had become apparent around the beginning of the twentieth century. It has occurred mainly among the children and young people of the so-called Western nations of North America and Europe, and also in some of the Latin American countries. This is the astonishing fact that children in these countries seem to grow and develop much more quickly nowadays than they did up to the middle of the nineteenth century. The following remarks appeared in a 1956 issue of *The Lancet*:

> It has now been clearly shown that in Western Europe and America children of all ages have been getting bigger during the past 50 years. Almost certainly this trend has been going on for as much as a century, but the first adequate comparison that was possible was between the years 1883 and 1938 for Swedish children aged eight to 18. Over these 50 years, children of age nine, for example, increased in height at the rate of about ¾ inch (2 cm) per decade and in weight at about 2½ lb (1 kg) per decade. The increase represents for the most part a quicker growth to maturity. The child of nine is now physically, and for all we know mentally, identical with the child of 10½ or 11 in the 1880s.[19]

These statements give us a clear outline of the problem in question. They have been further confirmed by extensive surveys of many thousands of children both in Europe and in the United States.

†The ideas put forward here are largely the outcome of discussions amongst the doctors of the Camphill Rudolf Steiner Schools.

Today it is an undisputed fact that the children of these nations grow much more rapidly now than they did a century ago.

Later investigations in Glasgow and Edinburgh showed that this trend had continued. In 1956, J. A. C. Keddie[20] analysed data obtained from schoolchildren in these two towns, who had been measured regularly since 1913. He discovered that during the 42 years between 1913 and 1955, nine-year-olds, for example, had increased about 3 inches (7.5 cm) in height and 7½ lb (3.5 kg) in weight. These measurements tally with those found elsewhere in Europe and America. This represents quite a considerable increase in growth within the space of a few decades, and one that is apparently still continuing. It is a phenomenon which certainly requires attention, especially since no one has so far been able to find a satisfactory explanation.

A comprehensive account of the investigations carried out in this field can be found in J. M. Tanner's book *Growth at Adolescence*. From it I quote the following:

> The data on heights and weights of children of school age show that the whole process of growth has been progressively speeded up, and that certainly by age five (and in all likelihood earlier) children born in the 1930s, for example, were considerably larger than those born in the 1900s. The magnitude of the circular change is very considerable, and dwarfs the difference between socio-economic classes and between geographical regions within countries such as Sweden and the United States.[21]

It also emerged that this acceleration of growth applies solely to the so-called Western nations — that is, to that section of mankind which in recent centuries has been the exponent of progressive historical development. The phenomenon belongs entirely to the West.

The increase, however, is not confined to size and weight. Physical and mental development has also accelerated, so that children today pass through the various stages of maturation much more quickly than did their counterparts a century ago. The older the children grow, the more marked this acceleration appears to become, as can be extrapolated from Tanner's description:

The American, British and Swedish data all give secular trends of very similar magnitude. The average gain between 1880 and 1950 is about ½ inch (1.5 cm) and 1 lb (0.5 kg) per decade for ages five to seven. The trend is more marked — about ¾ inch (2 cm) and 3 lb (1.5 kg) per decade — for the period of adolescence. But it is much reduced for the fully grown adult, with an increase in height of only a little over ¼ inch (1 cm) per decade. These trends seem to be continuing unabated, or at least they did so during the decades 1925–35 in America, 1935–45 in Canada, and 1940–50 in Great Britain and Sweden. They have been slowed up from time to time by the privations of war and, to a lesser extent, of economic crisis, but they were not slowed drastically or for long. The phenomenon probably started some time before 1880, because Roberts, writing in 1876, said that 'A factory child of the present day at the age of nine years weighs as much as one of ten did in 1833 … each age has gained one year in 40 years.' Kiil's excellent Norwegian data show little adult gain from 1760 to 1830, a gain of about ½ inch (1.5 cm) from 1830 to 1875 (0.3 cm per decade), and a gain of about 1½ inches (4 cm) from 1875 to 1935 (0.6 cm per decade).[21]

These data show quite clearly that the acceleration of growth we are considering started about the middle of the last century and is still continuing; if anything, it is increasing. Tanner goes on to explain that this is not merely an acceleration of physical growth, but that physical and mental maturation is involved as well:

> The difference in the size of children during the first half of the twentieth century was due both to an acceleration of the maturing process and to an increase in the eventual adult size reached. At the beginning of the century, maximal height was probably not reached until the age of about 26. By the 1950s, however, in high socio-economic groups in Western Europe and America, the equivalent age reduced to about 18–19 in boys and 16–17 in girls, with a height increase of about 0.5–1 cm per decade from 1850 to the 1950s.
>
> The acceleration of growth is also shown in the marked secular trend in the age at menarche. The trend is remarkably similar in all the series, with a reduction in the age at menarche of 4–6 months per decade over the period 1850–1950. Other European and American

data, though not quite so regular, agree well with these figures.[21]

Tanner published graphs that show us how drastically the period of childhood and youth has been shortened. About the year 1850, for instance, Norwegian girls did not have their first menstruation before the age of 17; by the 1950s the normal age for this was 13 or 14. At the beginning of the twentieth century, the average girl in the United States started to menstruate at 14–15; half a century later the equivalent age was 13.

The whole trend is alarming for all concerned, given the possible repercussions on the development of young people. But first we must consider whether a common factor can be found in all the associated changes.

* * * * *

The phenomena themselves are obvious enough. In the Western world, for example, this acceleration in the development of children and adolescents not only leads to a shortening of childhood and youth, but also produces individuals who are on the average taller than those who lived a century or so ago and who reach full maturity at a much younger age.

Personal observations of a great number of children have shown that children today begin to say 'I' of themselves round about the second year. This is an indication that the acceleration of development starts at a very early age. Unfortunately, there are no clear data on the start of the second dentition, and it is therefore difficult to determine whether this important milestone in the child's development also occurs earlier than it did a century ago. The data on the onset of puberty, however, have been fully established, and there can be no doubt that today's children are at least two to three years ahead of those who grew up around the middle of the last century.

It is remarkable that these figures apply only to Western Europeans and North Americans — that is, to those people who are most intensively involved with modern technical processes, and who furthermore have completely succumbed to the influences of modern civilisation. This applies particularly to the Scandinavian countries. Most Asiatic and African peoples, on the other hand, still seem to be quite free of this acceleration of development.

Many of the investigators who have worked on this problem tend to seek its cause in the greatly improved nourishment given to children and young people today. However, it has also been established that the increase in growth occurs without distinction in all classes of the population. The writer in *The Lancet* makes the following observations:

> In America, for example, the increase has not been notably greater in the lower social and economic groups of the population ... The secular trend is also much greater than any difference in the size of children in different social classes now or in 1880, so that if its cause is nutritional, it is a reasonable supposition that some specific nutrient and not simply calorie intake is involved.[19]

It therefore does not seem to be just a question of nutrition — and it is simplistic to think that more calories alone mean quicker growth and earlier maturity. It is also rather tragic to see how not one of the scientists has so far looked upon these phenomena as being anything but positive signs of progress. Children, they reason, develop more quickly and grow bigger than before, and therefore things must have got better. Such standards are similar to those applied to the experimental cultivation of grain and potatoes, and to stables where domestic animals are bred. The acceleration of growth in young people is not a result of breeding. It represents only part of a whole complex of symptoms that must first of all be considered in their right perspective.

Is it really such a good sign if children grow more quickly? Is it right that infancy has been shortened to two years, childhood to five years, and the period from infancy to puberty to only 12 years? Is it a good trend when youngsters complete their physical development at 17, only to enter life as half- or even quarter-baked individuals who are mentally quite immature? Perhaps this over-rapid development is rather to be regarded as a very dangerous thing which, if it goes on at this rate, may well lead to catastrophe.

We may perhaps be justified in viewing this tendency as one of the causes of the moral deterioration and behaviour problems among young people in Europe and America, and as a contributory factor in the enormous increase in juvenile delinquency. The headlong rush into maturity deprives young people of much-needed time, and their developmental processes become far too precipitate as they try to reach the same goal over a much shorter period.

This acceleration of growth must surely indicate the general trend of our age. The untimely haste with which childhood and youth pass by must surely be a reflection of the haste that characterises Western life in general. Perhaps we are right in assuming that the increasing speed of daily existence leads to accelerated growth and development. Yet what are the forces which have brought this about? Perhaps the introduction of railways, begun in Europe and America around the middle of the nineteenth century, influenced the vital laws of child development. Perhaps the development of telecommunications, and the gradual increase in the speed of all means of transport, have already had profound biological consequences.

Such ideas may well seem absurd at first glance. But can we altogether reject them? It is after all a well-established fact that some of today's diseases are due to our modern ways of living. We are quite used to speaking of the so-called 'manager's disease' associated with severe symptoms of heart and circulatory malfunction, which may indeed be caused by haste and restlessness. We also know that diseases such as tuberculosis and cancer are partly caused by certain factors in our environment. The poor conditions, for instance, in the big towns at the time of the Industrial Revolution can be regarded as a major factor in the high incidence of pulmonary tuberculosis at the time.

All this shows us how factors associated with the development of civilisation can have far-reaching biological and pathological effects. We would therefore be entirely right in asking whether the conditions of modern life have already had a noticeable effect on childhood development, and whether an acceleration in all aspects of daily life has affected the development rate of children and adolescents. Maybe one is consequent upon the other.

Certain types of precipitate development are known to occur in the biological sphere — processes that normally take a certain time to reach completion, but which suddenly accelerate so that they are completed in a much shorter period. The growth and development of plants and animals can, for example, be forced or accelerated by means of increased light or intensified warmth. These, then, are phenomena that are comparable to those under discussion.

The question, however, is this. What is the meaning of the general acceleration which is going on all around us today, and that affects the adolescent as well as the child?

* * * * *

Rudolf Steiner, in a lecture course marking the foundation of the Waldorf School in Stuttgart in 1919, made decisive statements on the necessary conditions for the growth of school-age children. In his 11th lecture, addressing future teachers of the Waldorf School, he said:

> You must bear in mind that the child you are teaching and educating has something else to do besides what you are doing with him. He has all manner of things to do which belong only indirectly to your sphere of work. The child has to grow. Yes, he must grow, and while educating him you should realise that he must grow properly. What does this mean? It means that your teaching must not be allowed to disturb the child's growth. You must not effect a disturbance of his growth; rather your teaching and education should only be such as is compatible with the child's growth. What I am now saying is of special significance for the primary-school period.[14]

Rudolf Steiner's statement makes it quite clear that the rate of growth in a child is an exceedingly delicate mechanism that is highly sensitive to educational and teaching methods. He reminds the teacher that he must teach in such a way as not to disturb the growth of the child. The teacher must become a 'companion of nature', learning carefully how his teaching can help or hinder growth and development. Steiner goes on to look at some of the processes involved:

> How can we gain an understanding of the forces of growth from the point of view of the soul? For this we must turn to a better kind of psychology than is current today. This better psychology tells us that

everything that accelerates the growth forces in a young human being, or makes him shoot up too rapidly, is related to a certain aspect of memory formation. If we over-stimulate the memory, we cause the human being within certain limits to grow tall and thin. And if we over-stimulate his fantasy, we retard his growth. Memory and fantasy are in some mysterious way related to the forces of life and development in man. And we should acquire the faculty for perceiving such a relationship. [14]

This description offers a vital key in the pursuit for answers to our initial questions, providing some insights into how growth in schoolchildren can be influenced by teaching methods. Let us now try to achieve a clearer conception of the processes involved.

Rudolf Steiner points out above that there are two entities in the soul which have a direct influence on the forces of growth: memory and fantasy. Elsewhere in the same lecture series, he alludes to the polarity of these two entities, tracing them back to the two basic tendencies of all mental life — sympathy and antipathy (Hans van der Stok explains these two terms in his chapter *Adolescence*). The power of memory is especially connected to the antipathetic side of the soul, whereas fantasy is linked mainly to the sympathetic tendencies.

Both the sympathetic and the antipathetic tendencies are intimately connected with the middle organisation of man — with his rhythmical system. This area is also known as the chest organisation, because it is where the rhythms of heart and breathing stream through the organism, and where the feelings are seated. This too is where the primary feelings of sympathy and antipathy dwell. Steiner explains that during the primary-school period (i.e. the second seven-year period) the child 'is growing and evolving by means of his chest organisation.' This means that, between the second dentition and puberty, the middle organisation is the place where growth and development originate.

All our emotions have a basic streak of sympathy or antipathy. The feeling of antipathy tends more towards thinking and mental activity, and thus towards the head organisation; whereas sympathy is more inclined towards will and deed, and is thus more closely connected to the limbs. If we place too great an emphasis on memory, then the forces of antipathy will be over-dominant, thus engaging the head organisation too strongly. On the other hand, the over-intensive use of fantasy will have too strong an influence on the will sphere of the limbs. It should always be possible for the teacher to regulate the activity of either side of a child's life. If he offers too much knowledge to the child, he overloads the child's memory. If he encourages too much expression of artistic abilities, the forces of will preponderate. Either extreme is unwholesome and should be avoided.

As Rudolf Steiner explains, fantasy and memory have a 'secret relationship' with the forces of life and development. He then establishes that overloading the memory leads to an increase in growth, whereas intensive fantasy activity retards growth. What does this mean?

At first glance, it might appear that just the opposite should be the case: an overloaded memory should retard the growth mechanisms, whereas the creative use of fantasy should stimulate growth. But anybody who has observed plants growing in the dark — in a cellar, for example — will have been surprised to witness the development of elongated stalks and panicles. By contrast, the abundant sunlight of the hot steppes and deserts causes plants to remain small and stunted. Lack of light elongates plants, whereas an abundance of light makes them small and stocky.

Similar processes are also to be found in man, although they function in a somewhat different way. The powers of fantasy are related to light and sunshine. They illuminate the soul so that the forces of growth are held back. So if the power of 'inner' light becomes too strong, it will impede growth. The forces of memory, on the other hand, are children of darkness. They therefore have a stimulating effect on the processes of growth, producing long, lanky people — they increase the rate of growth.

This then brings us to a preliminary understanding of the mental factors that can influence growth. If too much demand is placed on memory, the soul is darkened and growth is over-stimulated. If, however, the sun-like powers of fantasy are allowed to illuminate the soul too strongly, then growth is suppressed. Only if memory and fantasy, the darkness and the light of the soul, are allowed to work together in harmony, can the interplay of colour be achieved that is part and parcel of all mental existence. Too much memory darkens the colours so that they soon go grey; too strong a light makes the colours of the soul so brilliant that they lose their splendour and become white light.

The various shades of colour in the young person's soul are influenced by the teacher as well as the parents and other people around him. They are an important factor in his growth and development during his childhood and teenage years.

* * * * *

The insights provided by Steiner should now help us towards an understanding of the phenomena in question. We can begin to comprehend that changes in the environmental conditions have a decisive influence on the growth of each child. But if each individual is affected, this surely applies to the totality as well. General living conditions have changed to such an extent that they affect large groups of the population. During the last hundred years or more, this has certainly been the case for great sections of the world's population.

The Western world first underwent radical changes in its social structure through the enormous growth of towns and cities. People left the land, and industrialisation followed. This structural alteration of modern life is now a fully accepted fact. Our life is quite different from that of our parents and grandparents, and the change has been much more drastic than any that ever happened before in such a short span of time. The ever-advancing technological progress has continued to make a tremendous difference to our mode of life.

The world of the child has altered, too, and perhaps here the change is even greater than elsewhere. Even tiny babies face a different situation nowadays, since they are hardly ever born at home. Most Western babies are delivered in hospitals and maternity homes, and this brings the infant into a whirlpool of noise and anonymity from the very first day. Right from the beginning, life becomes in a certain way automatic and technical. Mothers take their little ones to baby clinics, so they meet noisy streets and shops as a matter of course. The radio booms everywhere, electric lights blind their eyes, and the noise in the streets grinds on day and night. I am not saying this to hark back to 'the good old days', but simply to present the situation facing the infant of today.

Infants are fed with vitamin-enriched and stimulating foods, while mothers and grandmothers are inspired by the false image of a 'big strong baby' who might pick up first prize at the next baby show. And so the infant grows up under a constant barrage of irritating stimuli. The infant's developing mind is stimulated from all angles, and he has to try to get used to an infinite number of impressions. The result of this is a development that of necessity must progress much faster than ever before.

In the nineteenth century there was the infamy of child labour in the factories. Today it is the constant roar of loudspeakers and television sets that continually whips on and drives forward the development of the child.

At school an immense amount of general and scientific knowledge is drummed into a child's head from the first year onwards. The mass of stuff which has to be dealt with seems quite amazing in comparison with 20, 30 or more years ago. Only a short while ago, I met a boy of 15 who had had a mental breakdown because he had been so inundated with study material. He had even been coached during mealtimes because the rest of his time was 'fully occupied' with schoolwork. Children and young people are driven to such absurdities by the pressures of modern life.

The powers of thought and memory are called upon much too early, and with such decisiveness that two important areas of the mind are badly disturbed. First of all, mental development is accelerated so that it pushes too far ahead of physical development. Secondly, fantasy is left in the background, and is not given its appropriate place in the child's schooling processes. Thus the forces for darkness in the soul are so strengthened that the light of fantasy no longer has enough breathing space, and cannot maintain the interplay of colours in the soul. Everything becomes grey from earliest childhood onwards, and physical growth increases accordingly.

Because teaching is much too intellectual at too early an age, a race starts between the child's physical and mental development. More and more subjects are squeezed into the earlier years at school, and things that were previously taught in the first year at university are now part of the upper-grade curriculum at secondary school. The specialisation of knowledge has made this necessary.

The child's developing body is spurred on by the acceleration of mental progress. It tries to catch up, as otherwise there would be disharmony between the two. After all, a subject suitable for the age of puberty cannot be imposed upon a body only nine or ten years old. The result is a kind of self-regulation, which takes effect as each new generation appears. The body races to catch up with the quickly unfolding mind. The darkness caused by the over-emphasis on the power of memory stimulates the forces of growth, and the body tries to follow in the wake of mental development as quickly as possible.

These are the causes of the disastrous acceleration of growth and development that can be observed today. The conditions of present-day life are greatly responsible for this, as are the misguided and wrong-minded methods of teaching and education. As the child's identity unfolds, he is constantly subjected to a battery of excessive sensory impressions, and his memory is continually over-stimulated. This accelerates the rate of development to such a degree that body and soul traverse their destined path much too quickly and reach their goal too soon.

It is scarcely surprising that signs of severe exhaustion appear at the end of this race. The universities complain about the inferior quality of their students, deploring the fact that they must instruct young people whose powers of memory are weakened and whose interests are simply too specialised. It is scarcely surprising that the educational level of our young people has sunk so frightfully low and that moral weakness is spreading so rapidly.

Here too are the reasons for the disastrous increase in the number of juvenile and infantile psychopaths, and for the many maladjusted children and young people. The lack of early fantasy development must surely have an effect, since fantasy forms an integral part of the mind. Neglected, it grows abundantly in the hidden recesses of the unconscious, and breaks out later in the form of criminal tendencies and all the associated absurdities. The discrepancy between the accelerated development of the soul and the more slowly developing physique creates an open gulf between body and soul, especially in those children whose physical development cannot quite catch up. The result is psychopathy and maladjustment in varying degrees of severity. Such children are effectively torn apart, and constantly fail in their attempts to bridge the gulf. They are victims of the conditions bestowed upon them by modern civilisation.

There are other symptoms, too, which point in the same direction.† During the last few years, a pathological disorder affecting children's reading and writing abilities has emerged almost like an epidemic. It is especially prevalent in Scandinavia, but is also found in Holland and northern Germany, making learning almost impossible. Between 10 and 20 percent of the children are affected. They no longer understand the connection between the spoken sounds and the letters — the printed or written symbols. This particular type of so-called word blindness (dyslexia) is spreading among the schoolchildren of the northern countries, rendering them unable to learn to read and write properly. One might even surmise here that a sort of self-healing process has begun in the youngsters of whole nations. The children, driven to utmost exertion by schoolteachers and scientists, by professors and specialists, are now beginning to resist their tormentors. The mind gives up, drawing attention to a problem that would otherwise be overlooked.

A further, more indirect symptom is the constant increase in the number of babies who are born with Down's syndrome. This increase began at about the same time as the acceleration of growth described above. It may well be that Down's syndrome itself acts as a regulator in the rush towards speed, as the children affected are particularly slow in developing. The learning difficulties experienced

---

† The assertions that follow relating to dyslexia and Down's syndrome have not been substantiated in the same way as König's main arguments presented so far. Consequently, they may appear to the reader to constitute a kind of offhand afterthought lying at the boundary of today's credibility. However, the editor has nonetheless included König's remarks because, despite the increase in scientific knowledge since his time, we are no closer to a real explanation of the subtle processes which contribute to the appearance both of Down's syndrome and of disturbances in word understanding. The reader will hopefully benefit from pondering König's thoughts on these issues.

by Down's syndrome children may in the end prove positive rather than negative, representing a healing factor in the vast sea of our over-intellectualised youth. For just by being present in modern life, people with Down's syndrome provide a means of social healing that brings a balance to the other tendencies of our time.

Only by surveying all these symptoms together and looking at them objectively can we slowly grasp and understand the present trends of modern life. The way to heal the associated social diseases was pointed out by Rudolf Steiner several decades ago. He gave a detailed description of a teaching method that recognises the child as a whole being and considers the important developmental stages. The Waldorf School Movement, which is now spreading all over the Western world, has put his recommendations into practice. One of its main features is a primary-school curriculum that gives the child enough time to develop and also allows sufficient space for the powers of fantasy to unfold. This counteracts those tendencies that lead to pathological conditions of the soul.

If there were more Waldorf Schools, there might be fewer Down's syndrome children; there might also be less word blindness, and juvenile delinquency might be far less common. But when one makes such a statement, people start to ask, 'How can you prove it?' And then one can only point out that everything described here has been made obvious by the symptoms themselves. Of course, it is impossible to show such things statistically. In this field one could just as well prove the opposite if one wanted to. But anybody whose eyes are open to what is going on today cannot overlook these phenomena and their true meaning.

The accelerating speed of everyday life over the last hundred years, the way in which hundreds of thousands of individuals are thrown together in huge settlements, the progressive mechanisation of our lives, and the resulting changes in the environment in which our children are brought up and educated — these are the causes of the alarming acceleration of growth and development in our children.

Having witnessed all this, we cannot do otherwise than shout out a thundering 'halt' at mankind. But will such a call will be heard? Will it lead to a decision to make radical changes in our present school system and then, step by step, to alter our social conditions too, until they are again worthy of humanity? This is hardly to be hoped for. But, in the meantime, children must be the objects of sacrifice so that mankind can be saved from running into destruction.

Bibliography

Note: 'GA' designates the catalogue reference in the *Gesamtausgabe*, or Collected Works, of Rudolf Steiner.

1 Karl König. *In Need of Special Understanding*. Camphill Press, 1986

2 Johann Wolfgang von Goethe. *Wilhelm Meister's Apprenticeship*. 1795–6. John Calder, London 1979

3 Adalbert Stifter. *Nachsommer*. 1857

4 Leo Tolstoy. *Childhood, Boyhood and Youth*. 1852–7 (translated from Russian in various editions)

5 Karl König. *The Human Soul*. Floris Books, Edinburgh/Anthroposophic Press, New York 1973

6 John Bradshaw. *Healing the shame that binds you*. Health Communications Inc., Enterprise Centre, 3201 15th Street, Deerfield Beach, Florida 33442

7 Thomas A. Harris. *I'm OK — You're OK*. Pan Books, 1973

8 Arnold Gesell. *Studies in Child Development*. Greenwood Press, London 1948

9 Rudolf Steiner. *Waldorf Education for Adolescence*. GA 302. Steiner Schools Fellowship, Forest Row 1980

10 *The Diary of Anne Frank*. (translated from Dutch in numerous editions)

11 Erik Erikson. *Childhood and Society*. Paladin Books, 1977

12 Carlo Pietzner. *Aggression and Boredom as Allies of Clairvoyance*. (single lecture 26 May 1968, New York)

13 John Steinbeck. *America and Americans*. Viking Penguin, 1966

14 Rudolf Steiner. *Study of Man.* GA 293. Rudolf Steiner Press, 1981

15 Karl König. *St John's Lectures 1958–65.* (typescript). Karl König Archive Botton Village, North Yorkshire, England

16 Rudolf Steiner. *Soul Economy and Waldorf Education.* 23 December 192 –7 January 1922, GA 303. Anthroposophic Press, New York 1986

17 Benjamin Fine. *1,000,000 Delinquents.* Gollancz, 1956

18 Rudolf Steiner. *The Inner Nature of Man and Our Life Between Deat* *and Rebirth.* 6–14 April 1914. GA 153. Rudolf Steiner Press, London 1994

19 *The Lancet.* No 6935, 28 July 1956

20 J.A.C. Keddie in *British Journal for Preventive and Social Medicine.* Vo 10, pt 1, 1956

21 J.M. Tanner. *Growth at Adolescence.* Blackwell, Oxford 1955

Titles by Karl König

Rudolf Steiner's Calendar of the Soul—A Commentary
Rudolf Steiner Press, London 1977
ISBN 0 85440 314 0

Illnesses of Our Time
Kolisko Archive Publications, Bournemouth 1979
ISBN 0 906492 36 X

Plays for Christmas
Camphill Press, Whitby 1980
ISBN 0 904145 20 4

An Easter Play—Prologue and Part I
Camphill Press, Whitby 1981
ISBN 0 904145 21 2

An Easter Play—Parts II and III
Camphill Press, Whitby 1981
ISBN 0 904145 22 0

Plays for Ascensiontide
Camphill Press, Whitby 1981
ISBN 0 904145 23 9

Earth and Man
Bio-Dynamic Literature, Rhode Island 1982
ISBN 0 938250 181 3

Festival Plays
Camphill Press, Whitby 1984
ISBN 0 904145 25 5

The Handicapped Child—Letters to Parents
Camphill Press, Whitby 1984
ISBN 0 904145 32 8

The First Three Years of the Child
Floris Books, Edinburgh 1984
ISBN 0 86315 011 X

Penguins, Seals, Dolphins, Salmon and Eels
Floris Books, Edinburgh 1984
ISBN 0 86315 014 4

The Human Soul
Floris Books, Edinburgh 1986
ISBN 0 86315 042 X

Swans and Storks, Sparrows and Doves
Floris Books, Edinburgh 1986
ISBN 0 86315 046 2

In Need of Special Understanding
Camphill Press, Whitby 1986
ISBN 0 904145 27 1

Being Human
Anthroposophic Press, New York 1989
ISBN 0 88010 280 2
Camphill Press, Whitby 1989
ISBN 0 904145 38 7

Man as a Social Being and the Mission of Conscience
Camphill Press, Whitby 1990
ISBN 0 904145 37 9

Brothers and Sisters—A Study in Child Psychology
Steiner Books, Blauvelt, New York 1991
ISBN 0 89345 271 8

Elephants, Bears, Cats and Dogs, Horses
Floris Books, Edinburgh 1992
ISBN 0 86315 107 8

The Camphill Movement
Camphill Books, Whitby 1993
ISBN 1 897839 01 4

On the Inner Path
Camphill Books, Whitby 1994
ISBN 1 897839 00 6

Eternal Childhood
Camphill Books, Whitby 1994
ISBN 1 897839 03 0

A Christmas Story
Camphill Books Whitby 1995
ISBN 1 897839 06 5

The Three Virtues
Camphill Books, Whitby 1995
ISBN 1 897839 10 3

In Preparation

Embryology and World Evolution
Camphill Books.
ISBN 1 897839 04 9

Animal Morphology
Camphill Books.
ISBN 1 897839 07 3